Star Children

Star
Children

The
True Story
of Alien
Offspring
Among Us

JENNY RANDLES

STERLING PUBLISHING CO., INC.
NEW YORK

Library of Congress Cataloging-in-Publication Data Available

2 4 6 8 10 9 7 5 3 1

Published 1995 by Sterling Publishing Company, Inc.
387 Park Avenue South, New York, N.Y. 10016
Originally published in Great Britain by
Robert Hale Limited, London
© 1994 by Jenny Randles
Distributed in Canada by Sterling Publishing
% Canadian Manda Group, One Atlantic Avenue, Suite 105
Toronto, Ontario, Canada M6K 3E7
Manufactured in the United States of America
All rights reserved

Sterling ISBN 0-8069-3856-0

Contents

Introduction

An Extraordinary Belief

In the past decade a truly extraordinary belief has arisen. It began like a whisper in the USA during the mid-1980s but has spread at the speed of rumour to encompass Britain and much of the world. It is so bizarre that it seems ridiculous, but it does have surprising things in its favour.

Firstly, it has not arrived out of nowhere. It has been gradually distilled from several decades of escalating and well-documented UFO encounters and, indeed, can even be traced back many centuries through the folklore of different races concerning fairy realms and baby 'changelings'.

In addition this incredible conviction is the subject of intense investigation by everyone from physicists to psychologists. They seek answers from the prosaic to the fantastic but hardly any of them would claim that they are close to cracking the mystery.

Equally, there is some hard evidence in support of these seemingly absurd allegations. Not only are the stories from around the world consistent in nature, but there are doctors, gynaecologists, hospital scans and some physical samples which indicate the possibility that all of this may be more than just a wild fantasy.

Just what is this astonishing belief? It is that an alien life-form has engaged in a long-term programme of genetic interbreeding with humankind. Moreover, that we, in effect, are biologically adapted and that our children are targeted, even conceived deliberately, so as to further this plan. It is an image not unlike that of a cosmic master race with neo-Nazi overtones; although thankfully with more benevolent intentions in mind.

The chilling thrust of this blossoming scenario is devastatingly simple. There are people living on earth who are both pawns within – and products of – an alien experiment. Some are aware of what has happened to them. Many have special powers to raise humanity towards a brighter new millennium. But millions of people may be part of this scheme with no more than a vague suspicion of something odd that once struck their lives.

We call these people 'star children' ... and you just might be one of them!

Jenny Randles
Cheshire

1   A Light in the Night

The boarding-house was dark and still and Chris was fast asleep. This was April 1960 and, at eight years old, she was worn out by the exertions of the day. Despite the muted noise of ceaseless London traffic creeping past her window consciousness was lost amidst a panoply of dreams.

Chris had never visited the capital before. Indeed, she had barely left her home in the Pennine hills and this trip, with an aunt and uncle, was the expedition of a lifetime.

Later she would recall the thrill of the fountain at Trafalgar Square with its aviary of pigeons. The guards that changed outside the Palace. Memories like these would all mix together into a nostalgic reverie that included steam-belching, blue-painted railway engines and red trolleybuses that were silently parading the safe and litterless streets.

Yet this night – the last of their short stay – Chris was in Finsbury Park, not a select location or inside a grand hotel, for her family were far from rich. But it had its compensations. Only a few hundred yards along the road was an old theatre and inside they were making a movie. Peering through the shutters had produced brief yet entrancing visions of Cliff Richard and the Shadows who were committing *The Young Ones* to celluloid.

Suddenly, the peace and tranquillity of the early spring morning was split asunder. Chris jerked bolt upright in bed. A faint humming noise now tickled the air, like a breeze blowing through a field of wasps. Beyond that was a vibratory feeling that powered through her body like a berserk pneumatic drill. Otherwise there was nothing but the light. It oozed through the curtains as if bleeding illumination all over the pillow.

For an interminable second it was magical. Then it became terrifying. Chris uttered a sound – not a scream exactly – that stuck in her throat. But it woke others in the room. As they stirred into consciousness the light disappeared. It cut out like a knife slicing through the silence.

The darkness had returned. The quiet buzz of traffic came again.

Afterwards, Chris relegated this experience to the back of her mind. It was a something or nothing kind of mystery. At the time she had asked her auntie, who had seen nothing, but who had used the vague placating words that it was only a thunderstorm. They were spoken like an incantation – trying to dispossess the monster. But they were trivial in comparison with the awesome power, and the brilliance, of that pulsing, resonating light.

Besides that, Chris had lain awake for hours after the light had gone. There was no thunder, no rain, no lightning – indeed nothing to suggest that the truth was as proposed to her. And yet for an eight-year-old that explanation was wonderfully comforting – and so it was accepted with a welcome embrace and all other options cast aside.

At least they were until many years later, when the haunting memory of that brief incandescence returned from its resting place deep within the mind and said to her loud and clear that it was no thunderstorm. It was something far more fantastic than that.

Three years later, in August 1963, Chris was on another holiday. This time she was with her grandparents in the seaside town of Blackpool. Again there was a boarding-house, tucked away in shore around the back of the bus depot. Again there were vivid memories, of Beatles songs and Freddie and the Dreamers accompanied by limbo dancing on the sands.

Yet there was also mystery once more.

Chris recalled little of it. Only how at breakfast one morning everyone was talking about the light. The muttering chatter of the adults in the handful of families sharing the building was concentrated upon it. They did so whilst self-consciously looking at their children and lowering their voices whenever it seemed that any of them were taking note.

Chris listened, receiving a reprimand for missing a question from her grandfather in the process. Later she tried to ask her grandmother about the source of all the fascination and saw by the slightly furrowed brow that quickly reflected back that even now – grown up at eleven – this was not considered appropriate for discussion. Later, when Chris was a little older, that same grandmother did share more about the events of the preceding night. For this time the memory would not go away. The nagging sense of sheer importance lodged in her deep subconscious and ticked away like a time-bomb with a long-term detonator.

The Blackpool light had been different. It had, apparently, been more colourful and attractive to watch. It had caused several residents to look out of their windows and stare into the empty sky. Apparently at least one member of staff had ventured onto a flat section of the roof and gazed upwards into the star-filled night – in time to watch a pale pink orb float serenely into the netherworld from which it had arrogantly arrived.

Again there had been absolute silence. Again there was just sheer mystery left behind to titillate the imagination.

'It was just above the roof of the hotel,' her grandmother had confided years later. 'Someone even thought it had landed on top of us. They were all astonished by it.'

Chris never asked if her grandmother was a witness herself. She knew that, even if she had been and had wanted to explain, she would only have done so when ready. Instead something different was itching to be scratched by Chris. A question that simply had to be asked.

'We were on the top floor – weren't we?'

'Yes,' grandmother nodded.

'We were closest to – that ... *whatever* it was?'

The question trailed away without response. It had never needed one.

* * *

In the years between the Blackpool adventure and its ultimate revelation, Chris became captivated by space. She wanted to be an astronomer and bought a telescope to scan the heavens; although the rapid invasion by the armies of sodium street-lamps made this a thankless task in the Lancashire town where she lived during the 1960s.

At school she would daydream often about the universe. Yet she was sufficiently inquisitive (if not exactly fastidious) to make steady academic progress. Almost without thought she discovered that she was turning these images into a form of reality by way of writing.

Chris would sit up in her bedroom scribbling away into a 'borrowed' school exercise-book and after a few days had finished her masterpiece. It was a curious concoction, done for nothing but her own pleasure. It was as if it was an exorcism of a demon in her soul. There was never any thought of showing it to anybody as she had done before with other things.

An early epic, *Alice and the Roof Creatures*, had been created like this just after the London visitation. Her mother had taken that and showed it proudly to others. Chris was rather embarrassed as that had never been the point. It had merely been something that she felt the urge to say.

The Alice, of course, stemmed from Lewis Carroll's stories, which, along with Winnie the Pooh, had always been her favourites. But the rest of the tale was as original as it was absurd. It concerned a little girl who was sucked up from her house towards the ceiling where she was greeted by strange and tiny creatures who dwelt in some kind of invisible universe.

For a time after writing this Chris would stare into the blue sky and tell friends – bemused by this behaviour – that she was keeping an eye out for 'sky creatures'. Her friends nodded sympathetically and asked if she had ever seen one – to which she would at first reply, 'Oh yes,' before learning that this was the wrong thing to say if you wanted to avoid trying to explain the inexplicable to those who were sceptical.

Chris's latest work – three or four years after her first (for the very last thing she was from day to day was a writer) – still had that childish naivety but was somewhat better constructed. It was entitled *Sleep Can Take You Far Away*.

In this story, a young girl of about her own age went to sleep and then woke up in hospital with no recollection of how or why. It transpired that she had been in a coma for days or weeks and this 'time lapse' was just the longest of several that she had already experienced.

As doctors struggled to comprehend what was going on, the girl had another lapse of consciousness and this time was taken on a journey by an alien intelligence. She was shown planets in our solar system, which she had to correctly identify. These included a tenth one beyond Neptune and Pluto which scientists had not yet discovered. Then she was taken to another star system and introduced to deeper wonders of cosmo-biology, including several types of alien entities with very different perspectives on the universe.

The alien guides were not aboard a space-ship and were not, in the main, visible during the encounter. This was mental communication – a trip to the stars using the rocket-ship of the mind. It was explained to the traveller that her captors were explorers who attempted long-range contact with other life-forms in this subtle way so as to seek out ambassadors on each new world and help inspire the people to a higher form of consciousness.

There was a problem with this process. The contact could only occur when the mind was in a certain state of consciousness and that meant switching awareness off during the astral projection. Time ran at a different pace on earth whilst these mental gymnastics went ahead and, as a result, back on earth (or indeed whatever planet the said ambassador was from) the victim appeared to be in a deep and irreversible coma, perhaps for minutes, perhaps for years. But the friendly visitors always brought folk back as they searched for the right kinds of people to spread their message to the new world. Most of those whom they spacenapped never remembered it.

*   *   *

After writing this story, in about 1964, Chris put it on one side since it had fulfilled its purpose as a form of catharsis. She kept the green notebook until she got her first typewriter as a Christmas present when O-level exams loomed three years later.

In the meantime she had extended her fascination with outer space into a discovery of the UFO phenomenon. She read a couple of books telling stories about floating discs and hovering cigars, but the whole thing seemed rather jumbled and haphazard. A French scientist, Jacques Vallee, captured her interest with his methodical approach. She read his new works as they appeared throughout the mid-sixties with a lot more anticipation than her weekly comic-book. But even Vallee failed to solve the UFO mystery and she soon began to suspect that nobody ever would. Then other, more pressing matters of adolescent life began to consume her interest.

However, she did discover one thing in this reading blitz. The sightings in Blackpool in August 1963 had been witnessed by others. However hard she might try to wish away the memory of that night there was objective evidence that the experience had occurred. That was rather frightening.

She decided to type up her story – for no obvious reason. In doing so the character was altered from a young girl to a slightly older boy. Chris, feeling satisfied with this minor adaptation, put away the manuscript inside its green folder and it was not looked at again for almost twenty years.

Chris's story may seem trivial, indeed almost pointless. It is an odyssey through various inconsequential experiences towards a strange belief system and its subconscious mode of artistic expression.

However, it is typical of how many people seem to have been driven towards a lifelong obsession with the alien contact mystery; coaxed, nudged and goaded into specific directions by a sequence of events that took them somewhere that they had never planned to go.

It is presented here not because it is particularly unusual. Indeed this story is mild by comparison with much of what will follow in the pages ahead. In a way it is a gentle training exercise for your credibility threshold since far greater tests will soon confront it. But also it might strike a chord in the minds of certain readers because, if many witnesses and researchers are to be believed, this is how a lot of people first realize that something is amiss in their childhood. Their life has been taken over by an insidious phenomenon using stealth of which the CIA would be proud.

In fact, as Chris's story unfolds throughout this book you will be able to see how it develops from these innocuous beginnings towards a resolution that is both figuratively and literally far more up in the air.

That said, Chris certainly does not know even to this day if these experiences mark the genesis of a star child or are merely the hallmarks of either wishful thinking or some mild psychological disturbance. She is as much in the dark as you are about the meaning of all these things – fighting a rearguard action, as she always has, against the overt literal reality of what these incidents *seem* to imply when pieced together.

Yet there is a final – and for me more pressing – reason for placing the birth of Chris's experiences in these early pages. Throughout the book we will meet many witnesses from around the world, often with incredible stories to tell. They mesh together in strange cohesion, as you will come to see, but you and I will both share the same difficulty when considering them. Whilst, unless I say so, there is little reason to conclude that such people are not telling the truth – at least as they experienced or remember it – there is still a sturdy barrier erected. They were there and we were not.

However, that is not exactly true with Chris's story. You see, I know for certain that it is true because I am Chris – Jennifer *Christine* Randles.

2   Not of This Earth

I first met an alien in November 1975. His name was Gary.

The location for this extraterrestrial contact was not especially salubrious. It was a small hotel astride a decidedly smelly soap factory situated amidst the downtown splendours of Warrington. Not the most obvious choice for a moment of intergalactic history.

Twenty years later 'Gary the alien' is still quietly trudging the UFO lecture circuits near his home in Northamptonshire. But he has never had any significant publicity for his claim, nor does he seem desperate to secure it. He goes about a perceived mission with decorum and patience – despite occasionally interjecting the news that time is running short.

Most people who meet him will not have a clue that he is anything but a tall, bearded man with piercing eyes and odd philosophies who used to make jellies for a living. But – if Gary's self-conviction is to be believed – he is a good deal more than that. He says that his spirit is from elsewhere, inhabiting an earthly body (which he finds restricting). He is here to warn of great disasters looming ahead and cites mystic prophecies from dubious sages such as Nostradamus as anyone else might quote the weather report.

Gary has been an influence on my life in many subtle ways. Superficially at least, his story is absurd. But there are secret corners to his experience that have made me sit up, take notice and not be as entirely dismissive as my logical, rational mind says that I ought to be, not least when I sheepishly arranged to take him along to see a top scientist in London and was amazed to discover that said professor was unfazed by Gary's 'true confession'. Indeed the scientist candidly told us he had met an alien before and even felt that his pioneering work in propulsion system physics might well be guided by extraterrestrial hands!

I left the university complex that April noon and blinked in the harsh reality of the sunlight. I was desperately trying to persuade myself that this day trip to the 'Twilight Zone' came complete with a return ticket.

A dozen years later and a universe away I sat in the home of a 29-year-old woman called Jayne in a council house suburb of Manchester. With me, to steady my wobbling reality threshold, was Roy Sandbach, a fellow investigator whose scepticism was on hand to be injected as an antidote. I needed such a quick fix should I find myself poisoned by the lure of credulity.

Jayne was unflustered as she told her story, well illustrated by her latent artistic skills. She was a nurse in a clinic for seriously (often terminally) ill patients and had the emotional fortitude to handle that kind of pressure. Her father was an American soldier from Topeka, Kansas, a strange little town once blown apart in a US TV movie about nuclear war – and having passed through it I was not entirely unsympathetic. Jayne shuttled back and forth between the two cities and expressed her desire to quit England and settle down in the American Midwest on a permanent basis.

This chatter was punctuated with her enthusiasm for artwork and poetry, examples of which she displayed proudly with evidence of phenomenal early-life recall, e.g. talking whilst still in her pram at a few weeks old. Her dream life was equally creative – expressing visions of out of body experiences (or OOBEs), flying and floating dreams – so lucid as to appear real and offer occasional premonitions of coming events in her life.

I kept thinking, as she talked, that she was the ideal candidate for the new fad of the late eighties – the FPP (or 'Fantasy Prone Personality'), a theory developed by psychologists and hijacked by well-meaning UFOlogists to explain why seemingly ordinary, rational and patently honest people believed that they had flown aboard an alien spacecraft. An FPP supposedly grew with such gifted creativity that they often found it hard to tell fantasy from reality and could therefore mistake the former for the latter.

Watching Jayne it was easy to see that the psychologists would conclude this here without a moment's hesitation. She was the archetypal FPP. But on the other hand what right did we have to impose on her what we defined as fantasy and yet she perceived as reality. Were we right and was she wrong? The bottom line was – and is, as the argument still rages – that we dictate what is unreal according to the consensus view. The conviction that our version is correct and the FPP sees an illusion stems only from the fact that there are more of us than there are of them. But once upon a time a heck of a lot more people said the world was flat, not round. Thank goodness we did not assume that they were right on that prerequisite alone.

Amidst all of this Jayne had another story to tell. One winter's night in January 1986 she retired to bed around 9.30 p.m. as she was on early shift the next day. Because of the odd hours that she worked her body clock was in rebellion and she found it impossible to sleep. So she lay there, eyes wide open, with her thoughts stuck in the tramlines that perpetuate insomnia.

Suddenly Jayne was struck with a thump from some invisible source and she found that, in fact, it was the sensation that she often got when 'returning to earth' after an OOBE. Only this time she was not back in her body – at least not in her present body. Instead she was in an alien realm with hot desert sands beneath her feet.

Looking around, lost and bemused, Jayne found that she was on a small ridge. The realism of the experience was its most terrifying aspect. It was exactly as if she had been snatched out of bed and transported light years through space to another planet around a distant star.

The indigo sky draped around her like a soothing coat of protective armour. In it were several balls of pure light flitting about performing extraordinary manoeuvres as if laughing at the gods of physics. Yet – odd as these were –

it was something else that bothered her to the point of desperation. A mood of desolation swept over Jayne. She saw the lights drifting away, heading for somewhere, and could only think one thought – 'Why have I not been taken? why have they deserted me?'

Jayne explained that it was like she was a small child who had been driven out into the Californian desert and abandoned by her parents. An impossible distance from home, she was watching her lifeline depart – perhaps never to return – feeling the utter helplessness of her predicament.

However, there was more to the experience. A voice was teasing her mind, tickling it gently, embalming her with compassion. She felt images flash through her head at warp speed, unable to catch any as they flittered away. Yet each contributed a piece to a puzzle that was now embedded firmly in her deep subconscious mind.

Only one ball was left in the plum-coloured sky. It detached itself from the rest and headed straight for her. Unmoved she let it home in on her abdomen and was swallowed by the calming, soothing, all-embracing welcomeness.

Jayne sat upright like a rock, feeling the coldness of an alien Manchester night. She ran into her mother's room and poured out her soul. Two years later she asked Roy and I, as we sat perplexed – *'Was I once an alien?'*

Another young woman was struggling with the impossible some years before Jayne's personal nightmare. She had an added problem, a young child – aged two or three, if I recall – which she had to bring up alone. This was not easy for anyone, even in a small mountain town in the south-eastern USA. But she was facing it with typical resilience – at least, until that fateful night.

Now the light had come. It peeked around the corner of an outbuilding and drenched the fields in illumination. But more horrific than its inexplicable presence was the fact that it stole something precious from her life. It took time. Several hours were kidnapped from the bosom of her innermost self and snatched – God knows why – for a joyride to infinity.

The woman had only a dim recall of what had taken

place. There were fleeting images of strange faces in the night – small white or grey creatures – the ones often reported with that determined, sad, almost forlorn look about them. Beyond that there was nothing concrete – no hard memory of what had transpired. Yet there was a burning question etched into her being.

What had they done to her child?

In many respects this was a fairly low-key and typical abduction experience. We came into correspondence in the mid-eighties through our mutual interest in the 'cosmic rock' group The Moody Blues, whose music had sometimes touched on deep questions. By then they were better known in the USA than in their native UK, where I had followed them since 1968.

Only later did this young woman venture a few brief, scattered details of her living nightmare. I did not pry further, as it was evidently something that was to be told only when it was meant to be told and only to those to whom she wanted to tell it.

However, there was something else beyond the experience which I was beginning to find in all these cases. It was as important – if not more important – than the claims and counter-claims about missing time and alien abduction, already ten a penny. For her life was transformed by the adventure. She became a new, healthy, vibrant, lively person.

I could not help noticing her superb artwork, which she quite rightly sent to me full of pride. I further admired her outpourings of talent in the musical direction – lyrics that told of space, cosmic consciousness and universal truths. She even changed her name officially to Judith Starchild. She told me that it just felt the right thing to do.

This kind of sequel was setting a trend that nobody was recognizing. I later got a tape from an abductee-inspired folk group called Phoenix – a beautifully appropriate name. It symbolized all of those who had gone through a transfiguration by the fire of alien abduction to become something more positive and creative – writing lyrics that were spiritually inspired.

Indeed, there was also the story of Betty Andreasson from Massachusetts that seemed rather appropriate.

During the late 1960s she claimed to have been abducted by the small, grey aliens who had visited her home. In doing so they had put the rest of her family into a kind of trance or paralysis so that they did not perceive any time passing.

Her adventures were told by long-time and respected UFO investigator Ray Fowler in the book *The Andreasson Affair* and its later sequel *Phase Two*. His subsequent works – such as *The Watchers* – had taken the story onward and reported amazing things about Fowler himself. He was a man that I had never met but had long admired. It now seemed he was part of the phenomenon after long association with Betty Andreasson (who was now called Betty Luca). There was even talk that Ray Fowler may have been abducted.

However, at the heart of all this was the peculiar, rich and yet decidedly weird story that Betty had told about her initial abduction. She had undergone what can only be described as a kind of rite of passage aboard the UFO. This had involved fire, water and a giant bird – which when all put together had the distinct characteristics of the phoenix legend – the mythological winged creature born out of ashes into a bold new life.

Was it coincidence that this image of rebirth and transformation (a theme even famed abductee Whitley Strieber later expressed through his second book) was suddenly becoming so prevalent in the 1980s?

The artistic creativity was another clue. Some expressed it through poetry or literature and others by penning music. In Betty Andreasson/Luca's case it was the symbolism of painting and drawing. Indeed, I now realized that one of her drawings had even featured in my book *Sky Crash* in 1984. At the time I had not known that Betty Luca *was* Betty Andreasson. But she had sketched for witness 'Art Wallace' (real name Larry Warren) the UFO that he had seen in Rendlesham Forest, Suffolk, during late 1980. That case again had displayed the magical qualities of universal transformation.

As time went by this pattern became obvious. A group of men from Glasgow had a spectacular UFO encounter late on the night of the Live Aid concert in July 1985. As vast sums were raised to feed the hungry people of the world by an incredible humanitarian effort via rock music, they saw a classic domed and glowing UFO drift silently above. It was in its brazen mode of secluded opulence – meaning that it was so vivid, so fantastic in its appearance that half the population of one of Britain's major cities should have seen it – yet, predictably, they did not. Indeed, equally predictably, it popped into the reality of Brian McMullen and his friends and popped right out again without revealing itself to anyone else.

McMullen and Co went on to launch their music onto the world as CE IV (a CE IV – or close encounter of the fourth kind – being in UFO parlance the term for an abduction). They have since performed at UFO conferences, had their music used as background soundtracks by the BBC in radio documentaries and perhaps made their most remarkable contribution with the concept album *Abduction* – for which they kindly asked me to donate some sleeve notes.

I was thrilled to do it. *Abduction* is a truly wonderful concoction, blending electronic music and enigmatic lyrics with pure emotion and atmosphere. From what I know of the abduction experience it captures its utterly weird and genuine alienness far better than most texts on the subject have even come close to doing.

The CE IV and the Phoenix stories are not unique in musical terms. There has always been a relationship between modern music and the UFO mystery. The Orb have had a number one album with songs written mostly on a UFO theme. The rock group Hot Chocolate had a chart topping hit – *No Doubt About It* – that describes a sighting they had in London after a concert. And the Carpenters had a big success with *Calling Occupants of Interplanetary Craft*, their anthem for a day officially designated to try to beam messages from this world into outer space.

Yet these more recent happenings were subtly different from their predecessors. For these were not one-off renditions of a culturally popular theme. They were life-changing decisions made by musicians who had gone through a transformatory close encounter. Just like those folk who were drawing pictures or writing inspirational text reflecting the truth about perceived alien contact, these musicians were doing the same in song.

Yet there was another subtle undercurrent rippling through these matters. The life change could manifest itself in less absolute terms, as it did with a young woman who told her story to the MIT symposium.

The MIT symposium was an epic event, to which I will return often in this text. It spanned five days in June 1992 and was staged at the prestigious Massachusetts Institute of Technology, adjacent to Harvard and just across the Charles River from Boston. It was not organized by MIT itself; their facilities merely hosted it. But it was largely the product of philanthropic millionaires and a physicist working in tandem with a leading psychologist. Together they brought over one hundred abductees, psychotherapists and abduction specialists from around the world to spend the best part of a week dissecting the phenomenon and trying to make sense out of it all.

This was a unique experience for me, participating as the sole British delegate. Not only did I provide results of my own experiments, but the power of this gathering was such that few were left unmoved and unexpectant. Two years on little really seems to have changed – which will be a disappointment to those who attended and expected such great things. But its lessons were invaluable and probably unrepeatable.

This particular woman abductee was one of the invited Americans who bared her soul to the audience. She told how in October 1989 she was taken by beings who seemed to know all about her, as if they had followed her life since birth. There was little conscious memory of what had taken place but she chose to change her name – just as Judith Starchild had done. This time the woman called herself 'Sky' – because 'it just seemed right to do so' and also because, as a word, 'Sky had a more healing vibration to it.'

Indeed, since around the summer of 1990, after the first abduction, she had made a sudden career change and become a healer – using positive energies that she believed emerged or were channelled through her to try to help those in need. Things had gone right ever since.

Later, Sky admitted in response to a question that she was getting positive feedback from the entities whom she thinks must have been in contact with her throughout most of her life. They considered that she was doing her bit for the cause but also that there were many other people who had been selected in some way. I got the impression from the views of the other abductees that they felt the real point was the raising of consciousness, that human endeavours were being hoisted by their own bootstraps.

This image of countless people selected to be one cell in some sort of major organism – growing like an amoeba and seeking to boost the quality of life on earth – was certainly an intriguing one.

Back in 1981 perhaps the best-known abduction specialist in the world had speculated freely. It is interesting to note that he – Budd Hopkins – is in his more normal life a famed New York artist, so also a part of the same cultural milieu to which these latter-day space mystics were drawn.

So convinced was Hopkins that there were far more cases of alien contact than ever emerged into the daylight that he had wanted to call his first book *The Invisible Epidemic* – because that is what he thought was going on. However, his publishers rejected the idea on the grounds that it made the work seem like a medical text. So it was retitled *Missing Time* and almost single-handedly created the now rampant trend to hypnotically regress people back to investigate suspected chunks of time that they felt were disappearing from their lives. In almost every case as a consequence they would discover unsuspected alien abductions lurking in their past.

So Budd was finding that there were countless more abductees than apparent above the surface – like an iceberg hidden dangerously beneath the pleasingly calm ocean. I was discovering that what mattered almost as much as these spells of missing time and pseudo-memories were the after-effects on the lives of the witnesses, who displayed artistic creativity far beyond the norm and who also practised healing, ESP, communion with others (to borrow another phrase later used by

Strieber) and blossoming spiritual awareness. As for the abductees, when they were being asked they seemed to see this as the whole point and – whatever the dastardly aliens got up to on their UFOs – to feel that they were gaining something tangible from the aftermath.

I knew case after case where this clearly applied. There were often points I did not mention to anyone but which fitted this curious pattern. Yet I had been as guilty as anyone of underestimating the importance of the tide whilst emphasizing the minutiae of alien contact.

Perhaps it did not matter what colour the table was that ET used to do his medical tests. Maybe it was very misleading to pontificate about the meaning of the laser instruments used to prod and poke around the insides of your body. Possibly other things were far more significant than all of that.

For instance, a family of five (two adults, three children) had encountered a UFO in a bank of mist on a country road near Aveley, Essex, in October 1974. Afterwards they had gone through a profound spiritual change. Indeed, ultimately the father moved away to join a kind of haven for spiritual drop-outs and started to create wonderful pottery. Aboard the UFO they had experienced a bizarre cross between literal reality and paranormal activity. Indeed, from their accounts, the alien contact even occurred in an out of body state. They had been floating in the air above their car – with their bodies still inside it down below – as they were given a tour of this alien world by their benevolent, tall, blond and blue-eyed captors.

Elsie Oakensen was another woman whose story I had told at length. As a teachers' centre manager she had encountered a UFO on a busy rush-hour road near Northampton in November 1978 but nobody else in the lanes of commuter traffic had shared this vision – at least not at that precise moment. Her adventure too was a more psychically focused event than literal alien kidnap. Indeed, afterwards she found herself interested in this whole area and, just like Sky, was delving into fields of spiritual and parapsychological endeavour such as healing. I have met Elsie often since – most recently in December 1993 when we did a TV chat show together. She is a wonderfully together and intractably normal person – light years removed from what the know-it-all sceptics perceive as spaced-out UFO buffs zonked by alien ray guns. It was evident that the positive things she has gained from her encounter all those years ago mean much more than the details of what may or may not have occurred during fifteen minutes of unaccounted-for time when her car engine and lights failed in the presence of a miracle.

Then there was the case of Paul Bennett, a fascinating Yorkshireman who had first got in touch as a child when he started to see strange things about as often as I saw the postman. UFOs, aliens, psychic experiences and angelic visions all poured forth from the netherworld of his consciousness. UFOlogist Nigel Watson attempted to unravel the meaning of it all, decoding his life through a sort of Freudian analysis in articles penned for *Magonia* – a magazine championing the psycho-social evaluation of alien contact. But maybe what mattered most was that Paul Bennett's experiences slowed down as he grew and channelled his energies more into a magazine he called *Earth*, which discussed spiritual and ecological matters. Finally he just quit and moved to Scotland to join a commune.

Underneath all of this spiritual badinage the story of Christine – in other words, me – was bubbling like a volcano on borrowed time that was not quite ready to explode. I felt the first wisps of steam begin to rise through the fissures when I realized that my lack of artistic creativity may not be as obvious as it seemed. What of my stories – *Alice and the Roof Creatures* and *Sleep Can Take You Far Away*?

Then Michael* got in touch. He was writing from London and was decidedly rational. He told me of something that had happened in 1969.

'I had a temporary driving job,' he explained. 'After a day's work driving around the suburbs I arrived at a road junction some two minutes from my depot and suddenly "came to" with no memory of the past many hours. This

---

* Here, and throughout the text, an asterisk indicates use of a pseudonym where not otherwise stated.

was a shocking event coupled with depression and feelings of 'alienation' followed by a powerful precognitive and telepathic incident.'

This was, as I had come to realize, a classic account of the psychic shock wave that tends to follow deeply hidden close encounters.

Michael reports that his paranormal episodes and vivid experiences were so profound as to alter his perception of the nature of reality. He was left an 'emotional wreck. I received psychiatric help and was once again a happy individual. However, I had changed considerably. I became a more loving, tolerant person. Now I felt spiritually awakened.'

Ever since, Michael has tried to rationalize what occurred to him as the outcome of his psychoanalysis. He has dabbled with psychological theories to try to explain the missing time and parapsychological phenomena that he has witnessed. Yet, in the end, he worked out his frustrations rather as I had done. He composed a 200,000 word esoteric 'novel' pretty much to serve as a catharsis for his own peace of mind. In so far as I can tell he has never attempted to market it. That does not seem to have been the point. I know how he feels. I did that too.

I regard other people's fiction as very much their own, so will not share the details here. But it is a fascinating allegory of the star child philosophy in which he starts to have communion with a ball of light as a small baby and is later befriended by a peculiar being who offers wonderful visions and voyages in return for his agreement to become a kind of ambassador – or 'progenitor of a new order of mankind' as he phrases it.

Michael told me that he prefers a psychological solution but has toyed with the idea of using hypnosis to dig deeper. I warned him that this might not help – indeed could even hinder – but the choice was always up to him.

This is not a dilemma experienced only by me. Indeed it is one reason why I encouraged British UFOlogists to impose a five-year moratorium on the use of regression hypnosis in the investigation of potential abductions. It was becoming the only accepted thing to do, yet creates as many problems as it solves.

Hypnosis stimulates fantasy as readily as it does recall. If you have someone – like Michael – who believes that he has had a strange time-lapse and who comes to UFOlogy having read books about the abduction mystery then the outcome of hypnotic regression seems easy to predict. Given that there is little way to tell the difference between imagination and reality – and the abductee themselves will be no better placed than the hypnotist in that regard – then the experiment may seem dramatic and exciting, but it is ultimately little more than that and dubious in terms of scientific worth.

On the other hand, if these people really need to work this whole thing out in some way to ease the trauma of not knowing, then what else can you do? That is why I give these people the facts – make sure they know that hypnosis is far from a magic wand – and let the final decision be down to them.

Researchers Melanie Warren and June Cameron from the Lancashire group FUFOIG (Fylde UFO Investigation Group) faced the same problem. A woman approached them after reading an article on abductions in a magazine. She explained that in spring 1987 at her home in Chilton, Oxfordshire, she had had an experience that defied explanation.

The woman was married with a young child and was a committed Christian. This caused difficulties in assessing her 'vivid nightmare'. In this she had awoken at 1 a.m. to see a bright light outside and, in a sort of sleep-walking trance, had got out of bed, gone down the stairs and felt 'guided' out into the open. Here she had been confronted by a huge object hovering silently above the road. It was surrounded by white lights.

The reluctant witness now felt herself being sucked upwards and her next memory was of being on a long table suffering a terrible pain as unseen hands probed into her body organs. She was paralysed and screamed in pain, but before collapsing into unconsciousness saw three small creatures that seemed to be indifferent to her suffering. She felt it was like a TV documentary she had once seen about salmon being caught, flopping about helplessly as they were tagged and then released. Only she was the salmon!

The woman woke instantly, jerking up in bed. The lingering pain made her get up into the cold. She went to the bathroom but was too terrified to use it as the pain from her nether regions persisted. Then she went to the mirror and dared look at herself. There was nothing wrong with her body and as if this released an evil spirit the pain instantaneously vanished. However, she suffered from insomnia for many days afterwards.

This woman was extremely fair and indisputably honest in the way that she put across her story. She apologized profusely for reporting it and wasting people's time because she had no evidence to back it up. The neighbours had seen nothing at all in the night. For all she knew it might just be a vivid dream yet at the time it had seemed so much more. She knew nothing about UFOs, save what she had read in the magazine article, and apparently did not know that her story matched so closely that of countless others around the world. She asked the investigators what she should do.

Had this case been reported in the USA there is not the slightest doubt what would have followed. The woman would have been regressed to that night at the earliest opportunity and few bookies would take any bets against an emerging full-scale memory of alien adbuction.

However, could we be sure that the result was indeed a memory and not a fantasy feeding upon a realistic nightmare and the cultural awareness that we all share today about alien contact? Aside from best selling books like those of Budd Hopkins or Whitley Strieber, almost every popular tabloid newspaper and magazine has featured stories and there have been movies (such as *Fire in the Sky*) and TV mini-series (like *Intruders*) which have emphasized the innermost secrets of the abduction experience. Who can be immune to all of that?

In the end the investigators decided not to pursue regression hypnosis in this particular case. Who knows if that was the right decision – or even if there was a right and a wrong decision to be made there.

One person who would believe that their decision was correct is Alan,* a 21-year-old man from Hertfordshire, who wrote to me in January 1992 to describe the experiences that he has had since childhood.

Alan has had dreams about UFOs since the age of six. They were very vivid and had included medical examinations and the taking of samples for genetic experiments by a group of grey-coloured beings. He had no awareness that such matters were a part of the real UFO evidence until 1990 when he first read a book on the subject.

As time went by Alan read more about abductions, particularly American UFO books that dwelt on the 'greys' and their experimental practices. He started to implant triggers into his subconscious mind to recall his 'dreams' more and more readily. As a result he began to get a clearer impression of things that seemed to be memories but had been previously frozen out.

In particular Alan recalled an instance when in his garden as a child. He was surrounded by small beings and somehow paralysed by them. A burst of white light exploded in the air around him, followed by another. Then there was nothing.

Later memories flashed back, like negatives suddenly imprinted onto his mind. In these he saw a strange object with wires on it and felt a vibration shaking through his body. One of these visions, on 23 April 1991, was so prolonged that it seemed real and felt real. 'I thought it must have happened,' Alan confessed to me about this.

Moreover he had found himself writing a sixty-four-chapter 'story' about alien contact and philosophy that simply tumbled out. 'This might just be pure fantasy,' he acknowledged ... 'Or not.'

When he first contacted me Alan was going through the usual process of trying to pluck up the courage to request help – i.e. hypnosis. This never happened, but were it as commonplace and freely entered into as it is in the USA then he probably would have been locked into an alien abduction scenario already by the time he changed his mind. That was in March 1992.

Now Alan contacted me again to say that he had decided most of his dreams were not real alien contacts after all. He felt they possessed 'hidden psychological meaning, for example finding myself alien to the human race'. He assessed his story and felt that it reflected his own beliefs too much to be more than that. Perhaps even more instructively, he had found a note that he penned only days after one of his most revelatory dreams and this had completely changed the face of the experience.

The note described the dream as it really was. The story that he had reported to me some years later was different. It was, however, what was now established in his own mind as a clear memory. This memory had adapted itself with time in such a way that he had never noticed. It had made his dream more like the abductions in the books that he had read since 1990.

However, Alan remains completely mystified by the childhood experience of the lights and beings in his garden. Indeed he has had a series of flash images since which seem to further develop this recall. He has even concluded that it relates in some way to a peculiar habit he has had since a child, of staring at the sky and saying 'the sun is my friend'.

It is quite possible that Alan really was abducted and that his memories are now seeping through into his consciousness. However, this self-analysis of the process is, I feel, terribly important. For it demonstrates that the generating (or retrieving) of memories from the subconscious is a dynamic procedure. There is no way to be sure in this day and age just how much of a story is true, or tainted, distorted or, indeed, simply invented in an unconscious way. The reality behind an alien abduction memory – especially one provided by hypnotic regression – can merely be said to be somewhere between about 0 and 100%.

Yet stories like Alan's are coming to us in great profusion. Since publishing my book *Abduction* I have heard many. David Jacobs and Budd Hopkins, who have written books on the theme in the USA, tell me they get dozens every week. Whitley Strieber said in Washington a few months after he first published his best-selling account of his own abduction that he was already by then being sent hundreds, perhaps thousands, of letters from people who felt that they may also have been abducted.

In 1992 several surveys were carried out to try to ascertain the truth of this massive conviction. The Roper organization did an opinion poll survey and found – via fairly loaded questions it must be said – that up to 2% of the world's population might mask a hidden abduction memory.

That awesome figure was tempered only slightly by a survey conducted by mental health professionals which found that in 266 patients forty-three had seen UFOs and 1.5% had beliefs that they had been abducted.

A combination of several surveys of 1993 had lowered the figure to a more conservative one. But these still suggested – on a range of criteria – that as many as 2 million people in the USA and half a million in the UK are potential abductees. Given that UFO organizations – at best – have records of around 1000 abduction cases for these two countries between them this suggests an absolutely staggering number of secret contactees who are out there somewhere – unsuspected, perhaps even unsuspecting. Yet, according to the testimony of those who have come forward, these unseen millions may be the pawns in an alien plan to change the world.

They are, in effect, the star children.

Of course, there seems a world of difference between having a dream (that may, or may not, be a dream) where you once saw some aliens and professing the belief that you yourself are in some way alien to the human race. But that dividing line is thinner than it seems.

Fred wrote to me from a small town in New England, on America's north-east coast. He is professionally an artist but has a background in psychic phenomena, which he has often used to help others. However, the most extraordinary things that have occurred to him began at the age of three when he started to have 'dreams' (the quote marks are his) which were extremely lucid. He recalls the first one well – indeed he says that it has 'haunted me all my life'. In fact he has researched pre-school children's dreams, alien abductions, psychology and lucid dreams states trying to find an explanation. He has failed but on balance has concluded that some form of intervention by another intelligence is probably involved.

In Fred's recollection he was awoken in his bedroom by a strange being who walked through the wall as if it were not there. The being was about six feet tall with large eyes and wore a silvery jumpsuit. In his hand was a rod with buttons on it that was later explained to be a mode of transport. It 'caused a kind of sleep and directed psychic energies for communication'.

The being took Fred through the wall and his world melted away and was replaced by an alien environment. He was told that he was being taken to see his real father, even though Fred had a very close family relationship which has persisted ever since and had no overt need for a substitute parent.

A similar being to his guide had lifted him up, as one would a child, and told a gathering of male and female aliens that this was his son. He elaborated in detail to Fred, eventually explaining what this was all about.

His earth parents had been selected but he was (in a way not explained) one of them. He was by no means the only one. These beings were 'guardians' and were always in contact but not directly. Their children on earth would grow normally but had tasks to perform and, at some future date when a major event was to occur, all of the star children would suddenly know who they were and would be able to communicate with one another.

The whole essence of this long and complex experience was difficult for Fred to comprehend at the age of three and he has gradually assimilated it as time has gone by. But he knew as it happened that these were intensely spiritual beings and their purpose was benevolent.

As Fred said to me: 'This event has made me ask many questions. It frightens me to think that I may have been abducted, or tampered with, worst of all, that I might be one of their "hybrids" – I keep wondering if some "program" unknown to me, is directing me, or waiting to go off ... I cannot explain this ... I feel something is happening. Yet I am just an average person.'

Yet normality is at the heart of the ever-growing mystery of the star children. Even if the stories that emerge from these ordinary people are anything but mundane.

3   Through the Eyes of a Child

I remember the valley well. The green fields sloped upwards towards broken stone walls and the little becks tumbled over the jagged rocks as they trickled downwards onto Bacup and Waterfoot.

I was born and raised in this area of Pennine moorland, where Lancashire slips imperceptibly into Yorkshire. I would love to walk up at the back of our house at Stacksteads on the tracks that climbed towards the heavens. The air was unpolluted then, or so it seemed, the summers never ending. And the sky went on forever above the slanting greenery and millstone grit that was liberally strewn with rocks.

They shot the wonderful black-and-white movie *Whistle Down the Wind* around here. It is hard to know whether the story, of a young Hayley Mills meeting a stranger in a barn and believing him to be angelic – perhaps even Jesus – meant more on its own or as a reminder of the places I could call my home. But it caught the mood of the Rossendale Valley perfectly.

Manchester was only twenty miles to the south of this oasis. But it could just as well have been on another planet in those days before motorways and traffic jams and when telecommunications were at best intermittent.

However, the Rossendale Valley hid darker secrets too, ones that at the time I knew nothing about. It was – arguably – the UFO capital of Britain. Today I cannot help wondering if it is pure coincidence that this small rural place where I was born and raised has – since I have left it for the city – attracted such a weird reputation. It is a delightful irony if nothing else.

It was here that I – or rather here that Christine – saw a UFO for the first time. I say Christine, because for years I

have fought back the memory as if it really was another
person who had experienced that day. But I know that it
was real. I just don't know what it means.

One day, when I was maybe three, I was with my
grandfather on the winding track that led to the south of
the railway line into Bacup. Down below the gentle
clattering of a steam-train on its way to Clough Fold was
the only sound that filled the valley. Otherwise I was
drinking in the silence and the wonder of a world where
everything was new to me.

Suddenly there was a dark shape ahead. It was like a
pencil in the sky – long, thin and sleek – almost as if
Concorde had been displaced thirty years through time.
The image was fleeting. One moment it was there, the
next it was gone. But I stood on a little rock gazing up at it
and gawping. Then I asked what the 'big bird' was and my
grandfather smiled.

'Not a bird,' he nodded in his rich Lancastrian accent.
'Not a bird.'

As we walked back down towards the main road and
civilization, time seeped back into our lives like water
soaking into blotting-paper. But I paused, tugging my
grandfather's hand and asking him what it was that I was
staring at. For on the ground, beneath the spot where the
big black bird had flown, was a piece of rock that was
shiny and peculiar. Back then it was just a mystery for
which I had no answer. Now, in the snapshot viewfinder
of my memory, it is obvious that it was a vitrified chunk of
quartz-ridden stone. Heat had seared it, even partly
melted it, and left it cast before our feet. But heat from
where? Heat from what?

I picked up a piece. It was slightly warm and tingling so
I dropped it, watching it shatter into fragments. Jumping
back quickly I voiced my wonder at this sight. 'What is it?'
I asked.

My grandfather, a staunch Labour man who had
survived the trench battles of the First World War with
some of his hand blown away, was never one to mince
words.

'It's part of t' sky,' he told me calmly. 'A piece of it 'as
fallen off. Leave it where it is and let's go 'ome.'

I believed every word that he said.

* * *

Later – years later, in fact – when I began to understand about UFOs, I had asked him of that day. He had forgotten it. But he had not forgotten the big birds. They were frequent fliers in the valley. He had seen one once near Whitewell Bottom as it sailed silently and majestically overhead.

'Folk said it were an airplane goin' into Leeds,' he grimaced. 'It weren't,' was all he had to add.

Again, much later, I realized that what we saw that day in the mid-1950s had been near a quarry at Bacup that was haunted by spaceships.

In February 1979 a call in the middle of the night to my home in Manchester had first alerted me to that knowledge. The caller was Mike Sacks, a tailor from Stacksteads who was a stranger but had my number via Jodrell Bank space centre, for whom I sometimes fielded UFO calls.

Mike had been up looking after his young son who had been sick when odd lights had poured through the window. Gazing out they had all seen a magnificent domed object descending into the Bacup quarry. The wonder of the valley had returned.

Mike rushed off to awaken a relative who owned a camera and returned to the site. But when he got back the UFO was gone. Or at least it seemed to have gone. However, two police officers were waiting for him, probing the night with their flashlight beams and looking a bit like Darth Vader wielding light sabres. They had been on the road that runs through the valley when a huge orange light had flooded above. They saw it head for the disused quarry and made their way up the steep track. Like Mike they felt that it had to be in there – waiting for them. Like him they were disappointed that it was not.

But there had been something there, lurking in the excavations – a strange hut-like object on the ground. Mike recalls walking past it in the dark and turning away with his mind echoing the word 'portacabin'. This was just a portable cabin used by workmen. Nothing to pay attention to.

Only it wasn't. As all had suspected, the quarry was not in use any more. The cold winter morning that greeted Mike's return to this hillside spot had confirmed the truth. There were no workers operating there, no buildings, no portacabins. Nothing. Whatever Mike had seen a few hours earlier had disappeared into thin air.

Nor was that the only time that Bacup police chased UFOs. Reports came thick and fast. In March 1966 an object even hovered over the police station and interfered with radio communications. That same stone-built façade was later used (as indeed was much of the valley and surrounding moors) as the fictional police HQ in 'Hartley', the setting for *Juliet Bravo* – the long-running popular BBC TV series about a woman police chief. They even featured one episode about UFOs, such was the strength of the local legend.

Eventually the sightings in the area became so intense that the *Rossendale Free Press* dubbed this region 'UFO Alley'.

A real-life Juliet Bravo wrote to me from Bacup in 1991 to add one more tale to the ever-growing pile. Juliet was not her name, of course, but it will serve well enough since it describes her bravery in coming forth to lay such information before a disbelieving public.

As a child Juliet had lived on an estate astride the edge of the Pennines heading out towards Todmorden. This was about 1973 and she was – just as Christine had been – aged three, almost four.

She explained how she awoke in the middle of the night

> to find the bedroom bathed in light. I don't recall any noise and have no idea of the time, as I couldn't tell the time at that age. I remember going to the window which was where the light came from and looking out. I saw three large orangey-white lights in a triangle formation only about a metre or so from the outside of the window.

Juliet stared at the lights as if they were Christmas tree baubles and then remembers nothing until she was waking up next morning excitedly telling her mother of the experience. She was advised not to be so silly.

Then she added something to her saga which made me sit up and pay attention for it again forged a weird link in a chain of events building towards something wonderful. Her life had changed dramatically after the encounter with the light.

She had not gone to pre-school or nursery but she

picked things up amazingly fast. It was as if her learning curve had been booted into orbit by the light in the night. By the time she started school a favourite party trick of the family was to get her to stun visitors by reading articles from the *Bacup Echo* just as she might if she were an adult.

There was more. She had to visit a doctor soon after the light appeared because she developed peculiar hard skin on a middle finger-tip as if someone had been needling it or it was burnt and it had reacted to that. Moreover she had to visit a specialist in Burnley around the same time as she was suffering from unusual trouble with her waterworks. The doctor said that it was a particularly serious case for a child so young.

As Juliet said, 'I'm probably reading far too much into these events and linking them with the UFO without any proof.' Or was she ...?

Why was I so intrigued by all of this? Because I recalled something that my mother had once told me – ironically as we watched an episode of *Juliet Bravo* in about 1981. This had featured a scene outside our old house on a sloping rise off the main road at Stacksteads. It was a decade before the real-life Juliet had written to tell me of her story.

Mum pointed to a wall beside a school and said that I used to sit on there. When? I had enquired, to be told it was when I was about three. I too had been able to read unusually well at that age, but more strange was the way in which passers-by on the street would scuttle past because I would look at them in the way that only adults normally do. One or two became quite perturbed, apparently, by the knowing looks that I gave them. I have to say that I have no conscious recall of this strange behaviour – thankfully. It does sound rather scary to me.

For what it is worth, I was once (in 1987) hypnotically regressed by a nurse who researched 'past life' memories. This was part of an experiment I was conducting and was some time after my mother had told me the above story. Under hypnosis I relived my birth – apparently with accurate details – but found myself at a very early age, perhaps weeks, perhaps months, aware of the fact that I had a mission to perform. I did not know what this was but I actually said under hypnosis (feeling quite embarrassed by it afterwards) that I did not want to be born but went through the process because it was a necessity. There was some sense about communication and very little else. Then the memory faded as if I had caught a faint whiff of it on the breeze before it wafted away.

Like Juliet I would have to say that this is very probably nothing more than me reading too much into innocent matters. Indeed, in my case the likelihood is increased even more by the fact that I had knowledge of parapsychology and many of its doctrines.

I do not intend to argue the truth of any of this, merely to report what I experienced and what I have been told. As Juliet's story emphasizes I am not alone in this – but whether I and others are companions in some inexplicable phenomenon or share a self-delusion is not for me to say.

UFO Alley is not confined to the Rossendale Valley. This is its major component, but if you take the moortops east from Bacup you soon come to steep-sided hills hemming in the milltown of Todmorden. This is UFO heaven.

In fact, Todmorden has even featured in an ITV series (*Strange But True?* – September 1993) under the guise of the most UFO-haunted town in Britain. That was a bit of a deliberate misnomer to emphasize a point, since several of the cases featured on the show were actually from Rossendale – but aliens know no county borders and in this case the strip of Pennine moor that links Todmorden and Rossendale is the real focal point of unparalleled activity. Indeed, in many senses the cases on the Yorkshire side of the fence are even more incredible than those nominally in Lancashire.

The UFO world knows all about the famous abduction of police officer Alan Godfrey, apparently snatched from his patrol car on Burnley Road just outside Todmorden on a November morning in 1980. It is considered one of the top fifty alien abduction cases on record, according to a survey by folklorist Dr Eddie Bullard working at Indiana University.

However, Alan's case is far from unique. Within a five-mile radius of the town I have investigated at least another four abductions. This, along with the countless close encounters and lights in the night-time sky, is the reason why Todmorden and Rossendale are singled out for attention. Many places can lay claim to be a source of UFO sightings. Few have the pedigree of alien contacts that this small moorland region supports.

Another impressive case involved Jenny, who was walking down the valley slopes at Walsden – actually the village where Alan Godfrey (unbeknownst to her) was then the bobby on the beat. This was November 1978, two years before his experience, so she was not primed to see something by what later happened to him. Equally, as her case received no publicity, nor was Alan Godfrey in any way dependent upon Jenny's close encounter. Indeed all of the other alien contacts that I know from this area have also not generated media attention. Most witnesses prefer to treat this experience as a private matter – not something to sell to the tabloids to give folk a giggle over their Sunday lunch.

Jenny's encounter is rich in metaphor. She told how her dog alerted her to the lens-shaped object surrounded by silver-green mist. How this huge thing hovered above her like an angelic observer before it split apart into balls of light that rushed two ways across the sky. As it loomed above her there was what Whitley Strieber later aptly called a 'communion' between them both. Jenny told me she felt 'joined at the soul' with the UFO. When it left she wept inconsolably as if she had just lost her very best friend.

Yet there was something more interesting to me that linked Alan Godfrey and Jenny together. They both shared a minor quirk that I was hearing more and more often from witnesses who went on to have alien contacts later in life. As children they had both had *psychic toys*.

I used this term as a fairly neutral one so as not to lead witnesses on about the nature of these things. But in fact psychic toys are very specific in appearance and behaviour. They are balls of light – between tennis-ball and basketball in size – which enter the bedroom of the youngster and quite often start to 'play' with them.

In Alan Godfrey's case he had recalled as a vivid dream when hypnotically regressed that as a young child this ball of light had entered the room and flown about. It seems that he suffered a whole series of odd nocturnal experiences which included several other periods of time disappearing from his recall. His youthful adventure was unexplored, but it was dramatic.

Jenny, knowing nothing of this story, when asked about her childhood told how strange balls of light would often enter her room and float about. She was not perturbed by them. In fact she sensed a good feeling in connection. Once or twice she called her parents in to view this 'fire' but the lights always vanished before they got there.

In Jenny's case, as in most others that I have come across, these appearances happened between the ages of about three and eight years old – in fact, often they ended even younger than that. They very rarely persisted into the teenage years or adulthood; although I have found one or two cases where even that was alleged.

The reason I called these things psychic toys was because that seemed to be their function. Just as children use toys or dolls to develop social and motor skills, so these balls of light were stretching their mind and their acceptance of paranormal phenomena. They may even have been training the youngster in psychic abilities – since it was clear that, whatever alien contacts prove to be, they involve parapsychological forms of contact. The aliens always commune by telepathy. They often have the ability to float or pass through walls. Out of body sensations are quite commonplace.

Even Mike Sacks had experienced this. He told me of what his brother called 'Mike's green opal', which had floated outside the bedroom window. It was a few inches in diameter and consisted of tiny, pulsing green horseshoe shapes. Mike had related to it in a semi-trance-like state.

These things overflow within the alien contact experience. They are undeniably important to our evaluation of its meaning. But few researchers are looking for odd patterns or links like this.

Marie from Nottinghamshire wrote to tell me what happened to her in about 1967 when she was aged seven.

'I used to really look forward to going to bed as I had some playmates. These playmates as I will call them were beautiful lights.'

She added that she could never get her sister to wake up to see them and she felt unable to talk to her parents because they were 'private'. They were vivid colours, with little speckles inside, sometimes with a haze around them.

One in particular 'was like a small football, brilliant white, and it used to come into my bedroom and just bounce around me'.

She says, 'I can remember wondering what they were but it never bothered me because I was never frightened of them.' Once or twice she stood by the window and watched them bound along the garden and through the closed window. She also saw them disappear that way, merging together and rising into the air where they would simply melt away. When they finally left her for good she was sad.

You will not be surprised to learn that as Marie grew older she also had further and deeper experiences.

She has had her bedroom flooded with light from the sky in the way that seems to precede an abduction. She has had vivid dreams of being sucked up into the air and finding herself inside a strange room where odd little creatures are fussing about her. Most interestingly, she now has two young children of her own and has seen lights briefly in the bedroom again – only this time they seem to be directed at her daughters, not at her!

Nor is this a British foible. The psychic toys are everywhere. A particularly good account of one comes from Dr Irene Scott, now a physiologist at the Ohio State University medical school. The experience occurred about July 1951 in her bedroom on a farm at Galena, Ohio, and both Irene and her sister Sue (then aged six) were witnesses.

She relates how she 'slowly awakened to see a small glowing object flying around the room. In color and appearance it resembled incandescent metal'. She watched it for several minutes spiralling around and displaying apparent intelligence. She then fled down-stairs, only to bump into her sister, whom she thought was fast asleep. Sue had seen it too.

Sceptics have suggested ball lightning in cases such as these. Certainly that phenomenon can appear as tiny balls and drift around rooms, but not repeatedly week after week or for minutes at a time. In any case, as Dr Scott points out, there was no appropriate weather that summer night and the light did not follow the electrical wiring system of the bedroom as ball lightning, being electrical in nature, is prone to do.

Cynthia Hind investigated another case from Chipinge in Zimbabwe, Africa. This occurred on 1 April 1988 but was certainly not an April fool's joke.

The witness, Caroline, describes the peculiar atmosphere to the room prior to the event. 'Everything was silent,' she says. 'Even the crickets had stopped their chirping. I felt cut off from everyone.' This isolation sensation is another extremely common prequel to an alien contact. I call it the Oz Factor and I think it represents a shift in the state of consciousness of the witness, preparing them to tune out environmental awareness and tune in towards the source of alien communication.

The fluorescent white ball came through the ceiling of the bedroom and began to radiate beams of light around it like feelers. Caroline was paralysed – either with fear or some kind of muscle control. Following her line of sight she could see the ball, now around her feet, with a shaft of light rising vertically up through the roof as if it was not there. Above it was a strange craft with several windows and a golden-coloured light.

She added: 'I felt as though whatever it was wanted to take me up in this beam of light. I may have risen above my bed but I did not take my eyes off this shaft of light so I am not sure ... The next minute I could see nothing ... It seemed as though I had been drained of all my energy.' She then looked at the clock. It was 3.35 a.m. Later one of her sisters, woken by the aftermath of this affair (when all the house lights went out as a whirring noise drifted away across the sky), said that Caroline's eyes were strange in the immediate wake of it. They were 'large and sort of glowing'.

Here, not for the only time by any means, a direct link is forged between psychic toys, UFOs and alien abductions. Quite possibly on other occasions the lights accompany deeper memories that stay unrecalled.

I am almost sorry that I did not have psychic toys to play with as a child. They seem to be one of the more friendly aspects of the alien contact mystery, helping to prepare the youngster for the more traumatic things to come in later life. Indeed that may well be another part of their purpose.

Dr David Jacobs from Temple University in the USA has made a detailed study of dozens of cases where abductees report the actions of the aliens who spacenap them from their bedrooms. Something that he found may well be relevant here.

He told the MIT symposium that the entities seemed to have a particular interest in human emotions. It was almost as if they could not understand the way we reacted to various situations because they themselves display a distinct lack of emotional response.

Consequently, there are many cases where a witness reports being shown images of strange yet powerful scenes – such as the birth of a child, mass destruction, etc., with the intention seeming to be primarily to let the abductors study how humans will react to this experience.

Similarly witnesses have reported being asked to do bizarre tests or to act out role play. One woman described a series of 'stage shows' that were put on for her benefit which retrospectively had the theme of 'humiliation', as if that were a concept quite alien to the spacenappers.

Perhaps the psychic toys also serve as a way to study the play characteristics and developing emotional skills of children, which appear to be of as much interest to the source of these abductions as any of their physical or medical experiments.

However, there are also reports of positive things coming from the balls of light. One case is reported by Peter Day, who is known in UFO circles as the man who took cine film of an orange ball of light from his car at Cuddington on the Oxfordshire/Buckinghamshire border during January 1973. It seemed to have been over a school at Long Crendon, where many children had witnessed the spectacle at the same time.

This case has been highly thought of for many years. Indeed the twenty-three seconds of film has featured in various documentaries about UFOs and I included a colour still frame on the cover of my 1983 book *UFO Reality*. In later years it has been accepted by some experts as more probably depicting a freak combination of ejected burning aviation fuel trapped in a thermal layer of cloud.

But there is an aspect to the story that is little known and which might be of importance in your evaluation of it. Many years before he filmed this object, Peter Day had a very close encounter with a ball of light that seems just like a psychic toy.

In fact it occurred in summer 1943 when young Peter was in the RAF and newly married. His wife was taken very ill and Peter was flown home from his base in Lincolnshire to be at her bedside as she could not be moved due to the severe wartime restrictions.

She went through agonies of pain and was suffering serious hallucinations. The end was clearly drawing near. But then, as Peter held her close, a sphere of light entered the room through the closed bedroom door. It was the size of a football and filled with smoky grey swirls.

The ball circled the room, came right up to the bed, then drifted away before leaving via the closed bedroom window. Within minutes Mrs Day was feeling better. Next morning she was almost completely recovered.

You may compare this description with other accounts of these small bedroom balls of light. Recall Mike Sacks and his sphere containing 'tiny horseshoes', for instance. A university graduate told me of the ball that she saw on the A681 between Bacup and Todmorden on 4 February 1988. She drove this route over the moors pretty often to visit her boyfriend but only once saw this orange ball above Tooter Hill as she crossed through Sharneyford. The interesting part is that she described its interior as being 'like a mass of swirling liquid' – another identical account. It was this internal construction to the light that made it so fascinating to her.

Another classic case concerns a teenage boy who observed a landed object with strange little entities inside. He was on holiday with his family at Machynlleth in mid-Wales during July 1975 and reacted so severely to the episode that he became hysterically blind for some time and required major medical and psychiatric care in order to recover. He also described how the phenomenon vanished in an incredible way, by becoming a mass of swirling colours (which he described as little blood corpuscles or jellies) and then blending into the natural colours of the grass and sky and disappearing.

There is undoubtedly an affinity between children and close encounter UFO sightings, of which these bedroom lights are merely a part. They seem to start the conditioning process that leads the youngster into a lifetime pattern of events where they share their lives with this alien presence.

Karen Hardman reported how when she was aged just eight (31 August 1969) her family lived in Gisborne, New Zealand. She awoke in the middle of the night to find herself staring through the bedroom window at a saucer-shaped object hovering over trees. She woke her brother, who was one year younger, and they both watched it fade away. Next day they told their parents and were separated, taken to different rooms and asked to draw what they had seen. This dispelled any thought that the whole thing was a nightmare. Their pictures were almost identical.

Jackie was living in Amherst, Novia Scotia, Canada and from the age of nine had countless vivid dream-like experiences with UFOs. Some were certainly real events. In 1979 she was out with two of her young friends near a baseball park. Suddenly a huge dark triangular mass appeared overhead, studded with green lights. Then, as Jackie explained, 'There seemed to be a memory gap. We saw the light drop and move towards us. We saw the object overhead flying away. But I do not recall the pieces in between.' Despite attempts to get her to talk, the one friend with whom Jackie is still in contact will discuss any childhood memory but the one about that night with the UFO. It is something that she, unlike Jackie, simply wants to put out of reach.

In June 1973 at Loch Ryan in Galloway, Scotland, a young man awoke at 4.30 a.m. and found himself with a compulsion to walk from his bedroom onto the landing. He did so and saw three orange balls of light lined up into a triangle over the water. They stayed there for a few minutes, locking him into this trance, and then shot upwards at fantastic speed. This seemed to break the spell and he came to with both his parents standing behind him. They had also been awoken by the same weird urge to walk onto the landing and stare out of the window.

Years later, a journalist who was interviewing me broke off to tell me a story he had not related to anyone before. He knew nothing about the above case but in October 1977 he had seen three balls of light lined up into a triangle hovering over moss between Upholland and Skelmersdale in Lancashire. They too had shot away into the dark night. Again they had a trance-like spell upon him, but with an even more curious feature. Two days later he remembered that he had known – with utter certainty in advance – that this encounter was going to happen. It was less a premonition than an absolute foreknowledge. Yet during and immediately after the encounter this memory had disappeared.

A youth from Bangor, Northern Ireland, reported another curious tale. It was in the autumn of 1976 and he had a young, rebellious brother. Yet for some reason that night this boy had gone to bed without complaint – rare enough to be noteworthy. Soon afterwards the house became stiflingly hot, even though there was no heating on. The witness had gone upstairs and suddenly became engulfed in the Oz Factor. All the sounds around him vanished. A busy road passed by outside and traffic noise ceased unexpectedly. He entered the bathroom next to his brother's room and spotted a bright white light through the blinds. It was coming from an oval mass over the roadway. As he tried to fathom what it was, the light rapidly expanded like a sun going nova and he was swallowed up by an explosion of brilliance. He added that this was 'the purest white light I have ever seen'. Yet oddest of all the light acted as if it were solid – almost an arm of a crane lifting him off the ground. The boy was raised up from the floor in the grip of this phenomenon and then thrown backwards with great force against the bathroom wall. He lay paralysed for a timeless period that he could not recount with bright lights flashing in front of his eyes, his muscle tone almost completely collapsed and his forehead pounding. Then he slid onto the ground like a floppy doll and gradually recovered his senses. In the distance he could see the light through the blinds climbing away into the sky. With it all sounds returned to normal.

This focusing on children was further emphasized to a young mother from Felling in County Durham, an area that has been rich in encounters with strange little creatures across many years. In June 1978, when she had a baby girl aged just eighteen months, she was woken in her bed by a buzzing, high-pitched noise. It vibrated through her body and was not unlike an electric shock. Her head 'felt like it would burst'. Then she found that an unseen figure was holding her wrist. She was paralysed and unable to move but could see that it had a fuzzy aura surrounding it. A bluish light was bathing the room. The worst part of all was that where the being touched her it created a weird effect like an X-ray plate. She could see into her arm, the bones and blood vessels. It was as if the entity were studying her. She could see the bedside clock in the glow. It read 3.50 a.m. Then there was a sudden 'reality blink' and the figure was gone, everything was back to normal and an hour had disappeared in an instant. She had more visitations in future and was 'told' that they were really investigating her daughter.

Nigel Mortimer reported another case on 15 July 1989 at Addingham in Yorkshire. He related how a woman got up one morning quite early and went to the shops. Whilst out she was told by a neighbour that at 3.15 a.m. there had been a strange noise like a vacuum cleaner in the sky. Going to the window the neighbour had seen a massive object with coloured lights passing from their vicinity towards Beamsley Beacon, a hill situated to the north. After returning home to convey this strange story to her husband he had a shock to offer in reply. Their six-year-old daughter had awoken at around 3 a.m. to see a small figure climbing the stairs and heading for her bedroom. Later the figure returned, along with a female companion. In their visits they never did anything except watch and then vanish. The girl described them as about five feet tall with thin white faces and unusual 'angry' eyes. She used the term 'fight creatures' and also referred to them as ghosts, never mentioning either UFOs or aliens in her

story. To describe the clothing – a sort of dark jumpsuit –
she said that the woman reminded her of Anneka Rice (a
TV personality who was noted for taking on game show
challenges and treasure hunts wearing one piece coveralls).

I could go on and on relating stories such as these. There are
so many of them. It is obvious that something remarkable is
happening, because such consistent threads weave them
all together.

Again and again we see patterns repeated: the motif of
the triangle (which again Whitley Strieber later picked up
from his own experience), artistic creativity, mind control
and evident altered state of consciousness within which the
encounter takes place, the psychic nature of the phenomenon where magic and illusion replace physics and
common-sense logic and, above all, the interest in children
– never malicious, merely curious, as if some kind of
long-term surveillance is underway.

Dr John Mack, a psychologist at the Harvard Medical
School in Massachusetts, finds these childhood cases of
great importance. He feels that they help dispel the
common sceptical argument that witnesses are conditioned to accept a cultural pattern about UFO abductions.
They know what they are supposed to be like from all the
media attention given to them. But children as young as
five or six are unlikely to be so conditioned by such hype as
to relate a story that fits so clearly into the adult stereotype.

Just one more case will suffice at this stage. It is
particularly fascinating as it involves identical twins. I am
not aware of any other case where this factor applies and, as
such, it identifies the case as one of significance, whether
the abduction phenomenon be perceived as extraterrestrial
or psychological in nature.

Unfortunately, because they wish no publicity for their
experiences (to a large extent commendably so as not to
attract towards them what might prove useful publicity), I
can say little about them except that they both display the
usual artistic flair and have shared in the close encounter
experiences since young children – even though one twin
has had some further experiences on his own.

The episodes occur in the home counties of England and

involve many things – such as seeing balls of light outside the window, once having a curious 'attack' from a buzzing object in the garden when they were both very young and, perhaps most interestingly, an incident in their house when their dog was also a witness.

It was a winter's night and dark. They were standing in the hallway when one twin announced that he felt very odd. It was almost as if an earthquake were striking, he explained. There were vibrations or tremors running through him.

I knew the feeling he was describing very well. Not only had it happened to me that night in Finsbury Park, London, but during childhood it had often recurred in times of stress. I remembered when I was trying to learn to swim and was deeply afraid as the sensation swept over me again. It was like my head was a hollowed-out piece of metal that was ringing as if it were a bell and writhing, not exactly with painful vibrations but buzzing, gurgling charges wriggling through my body. It is hard to put into words a feeling that defies description. This, it seems, was just what many abductees have described at the onset of their experience.

Of course, there was no sense of abduction as this 'earthquake' coursed through the body of twin A. He said what was happening to him but already his brother was feeling it too. The atmosphere in the house had altered subtly. 'It was tense and silent,' twin B remarked. Even the dog had instantly pricked up his ears and was staring into space.

Then a bright light appeared as a reflection in the frosted glass of the doorway. Simultaneously a small figure scuttled through the hall and headed upstairs. The leaves on a potted plant rustled to emphasize the reality of this experience.

Twin B saw this, but his brother, facing the opposite way, did not. There was no sound in conjunction, just the clear sight of a figure about three feet tall dressed in an allover black jumpsuit with a helmet covering the head.

In accompaniment the dog went berserk, before heading off into a corner and remaining there whimpering and cowering. Twin B was so certain of what he had just seen that he rushed to the kitchen drawer, took out a knife and went off in search of the expected burglar. Of course, the house was empty and all the doors and windows were locked. Only on careful consideration afterwards did it become obvious that this intruder was no earthly thief.

It is this focus upon children that upsets so many people – particularly mothers who are ensnared by the encounters.

Sandie, an American abductee, expressed it well. She explained that there was a desperate need for money, for understanding, for the right kind of caring people, to get together and get to the bottom of this mystery. She seemed to care less about the effect on her own life than she did about her children. The fact that she had been a part of this alien experiment was less important to her than the fact that the aliens had been interested in her baby daughter.

Indeed, her story creates a world record of sorts for the alien abduction. She recalls an incident where the small grey beings appeared in her house and took her son away for some tests, before bringing him back again apparently unharmed. They had spacenapped him straight from his crib and he was only six weeks old at the time.

I first saw this effect directly in action when I had to spend several hours calming a severely distressed young mother who was a complete stranger to me. She had traced my house through neighbours knowing of my interest. This was not widely appreciated at the time as I had yet to publish any books in this field.

The woman was burning to report a fairly low-key experience on Barton Moss at Irlam, Lancashire. It had taken place at 6 a.m. on 26 September 1976.

The flattened disc that she had seen in the dawn light had landed outside her back garden on open farmland. There was little more to it than that. Yet she had an almost paranoid fear that it was piloted by aliens who were after her young child, a daughter then aged nine. She kept asking me how she could prevent this from happening again.

In no way was she mentally disturbed. She was a rational, ordinary and typically protective mother who had been emotionally scarred by a sighting that in truth should not have had such a profound effect.

At the time I did what I could and assumed that she was simply taken in by the media obsession with UFOs. This had somehow exaggerated the episode in her mind. However, there were a few relevant clues about it. She reported subsequent dreams of floating and a sensation of being 'chosen' by some force. Today I wonder whether perhaps there may not have been more to this case than I ever looked for – indeed wanted to look for. Perhaps there was a reason for that reluctance.

I quickly realized from the details of her case that my bedroom was actually closer to the spot where this thing had come down than was the house from where this frightened woman had been witness to the UFO.

I went over her account of a typical oval with a flattened base, inset on the side with yellow windows which illuminated the clouds as it climbed up and flew straight over my rooftop at a height of maybe one hundred feet.

Feeling goosebumps I stared across the moss to the little stand of trees where this thing had reputedly come to rest for several minutes. Much later I dared walk out along the little track but could not steal myself to go any closer than that across the peat bogs. My bedroom was certainly the nearest place of any occupation to the spot where this UFO had touched down. At best it was several hundred yards away. I had been inside my room that night at the time as the drama unfolded – fast asleep, oblivious.

But could I really be certain that this thing was not after me?

4   Isn't Everyone Like This?

The young woman looked me straight in the eye. At least she tried to do so. But I could tell that her focus was wandering, her gaze blurred as she drifted back to the childhood memory that she had just poured out.

Susan* had described, in a rich Lancastrian accent, how at the age of eight she had floated down the stairs of her Bolton home. This was not in any out-of-body sense, but in a very literal reality. She had simply drifted off the ground to a height of a couple of feet and then sailed down the steps like a comic-book superhero. This feat had been witnessed by her brother, who was standing goggle-eyed in the hallway. Perhaps more surprising still was that now he was an adult, he was willing to affirm what he had then experienced.

I took a quick breath then ploughed on with the questioning. After a while at this game you become used to accepting ridiculous stories as a matter of course. So I just nodded politely, even though my brain was telling me one thing as my pen was writing down another.

Then the woman, in her early twenties, expressed in such matter-of-fact tones the aftermath to this bizarre experience.

'This happened to me several times when I was about that age, but then it just sort of stopped.'

I nodded again, urging her onward without seeming to be too committed to the truth of her story.

'Why do you think it stopped?' I asked.

Oh, I know that [she replied with an almost wicked surety that implied this was something she had often thought about before]. When I first started to float about the house I thought it was perfectly normal. Then my brother looked on sort of stunned and I said, 'But isn't everyone like this?' He said no very firmly with horror etched across his face. Then I realized that what I had just done was not normal. It was not normal in any way. After that it became much harder. Pretty soon it was impossible.

This woman went on to have a close encounter with aliens, in the way so typical of many others in this book. But in a sense her childhood adventures are rather more important, for they reflect a trend that stares anyone who confronts this mystery fully in the face. Sadly, all too often researchers fail to see the writing and, more usually, walk headlong into the wall.

People who as adults have alien contacts have, often as children, grown in life immersed within a sea of supernatural happenings. It is as if, for them, the paranormal *is* the normal day to day reality. The world of others is the one that is really topsyturvy.

I have noticed that researchers in the USA run a mile from this kind of revelation. They seem terrified by the dissipation of their phenomenon through psychic experiences. I think this is because they see it as the product of an alien invasion – extraterrestrial Neil Armstrongs landing on the earth in otherworldly space shuttles and saying 'take me to your leader'. For them aliens and ESP just don't make good bedfellows.

What this curiously ignores is the fact that every alien contact is steeped in psychic phenomena. Entities walk through walls, appear and disappear at will, float their victims in out-of-body states, chat with witnesses using telepathy and seem possessed of precognitive powers.

So this psychic track record of the witnesses is – not for me, at any rate – a dilution of the mystery or, worse still, a handing over of the baton to the realm of spirit mediums and spoon-benders. Rather it is just a fact of life that cannot be avoided, and we should not even seek to avoid. It is a very helpful clue that points us in the right direction. And clues are few and far between in this wonderful enigma.

We can emphasize this point with many cases, but a few will suffice to demonstrate what I am arguing about.

That children are special when it comes to that sixth sense is illustrated here by two cases.

Mike was doing what many young boys do, playing in a dangerous place. He had no idea it was dangerous. But it was a dried-up river hollow in Derbyshire and there had been torrential rain. Suddenly, a voice pierced his mind yelling, 'Get out!' He did, without question. Seconds later a flash flood swept through the spot where he had just been standing.

Lisa was driving with her mother near Cirencester when they found themselves diverted onto a back road. Suddenly she heard a motorcycle engine, but her mother, sitting right next to her, did not. Yet the sound was so loud it appeared to be immediately behind them. There was no nearby road from which the sound could have carried and her mother chided Lisa for having an over-active imagination. Perhaps so, but two or three minutes later, with the memory still fresh and causing their driving to be less frantic than it might have been, a motorcycle really appeared behind them, lost control and smashed into them. Luckily, there were no serious injuries. This awareness of a warning sound transmitted across time had quite possibly minimized the catastrophe that was looming. But only the young mind was open and receptive to it. Lisa's mother was somehow immune.

It is not surprising that children often regard such things as a sign that they are 'protected'. That protection is commonly perceived as being from an alien source and this is one of the earliest indications star children have about their possible origin.

For example, Karen from Cornwall describes how as a teenager in Warrington, Cheshire, in September 1976 she had to walk home in the early hours on several nights. As she did so she heard in her head a very distinctive female voice calling her name. She said that it was similar to her own voice but as if it were coming down a tunnel. On some occasions other girls were with her. But they heard nothing. She checked behind walls, as it occurred at the same spot in a housing estate each night. Still nothing. By now Karen was convinced that something was wrong with her. It had to be inside her mind. But after two weeks of this bizarre ritual she was walking alone after a night out with friends when a man leapt out from behind the wall she had so often peered fruitlessly behind. He tried to rape and strangle her and probably would have succeeded, but for the fact that as she struggled something miraculous happened. A brick materialized out of nowhere straight into her hand and she whacked her assailant over the head with it. He crashed to the ground, then staggered away. Karen was badly scarred, suffering traumatic shock that left her unable to speak for several weeks. After this she quit the area and went south. But she is certain that someone protected her from death.

Paul from Bradford felt the same way in August 1978. He was fifteen and for several days had premonitions of danger. Then pictures in his room began to move about on their own in some preternatural way and the sense of impending disaster grew. Finally, on 22 August, the chain on his bicycle snapped as he rode in the sunshine on a quiet lane. The wheel locked. Paul was hurled over the top headfirst into a tree. He recovered consciousness two days later with amazed doctors expressing great relief. He had severely fractured his skull and hovered on the edge of death for twenty-four hours. But as he lay there in the hospital bed a UFO had appeared in the sky overhead, as if a guardian angel was sending out healing vibrations. From that point onward Paul began to pull through.

These children had countless other strange experiences to relate, of which these specific examples are but brief interludes. Three of the four subsequently went on to have alien contacts – at least one of which involved an abduction, quite possibly others. The fourth may well also have had a track record of UFO experiences, but she never shared them with me if she did.

You can see how people like Karen and Paul, in particular, would grow up with a sense of uniqueness about their lives. At first, just as Susan did, they presume that such things are commonplace in everybody else – but then they realize that floating, seeing the future, hearing voices out of nowhere, experiencing miracles and the rest of the things that happen to them day in, day out, are not considered normal at all. Indeed they are regarded with deep suspicion if they claim them once, let alone frequently. This tends to force these children inwards on themselves, bottling up the psychic pressure and not sharing it with others. Time and again I have seen that manifested in various ways, but artistic expression may be just one form of letting the genie out of the bottle. For when the steam builds up it has to get out somewhere. It cannot stay inside forever or else it might explode.

It is worth looking at a couple of cases where we can trace highlights of a star child's development. There are bound to be things that we can learn from this.

Gwyneth was born in the early 1950s and brought up in rural south Wales. Almost as far back as she can recall she had 'vivid waking dreams', as she calls them. These involved 'strange people either passing through my bedroom or just standing and watching me'.

I have heard similar things from many who become abductees. One from Liverpool told me how as she walked through the city streets at about the age of five or six she would 'see' countless people – some with feet suspended in the air as if using a pavement higher than the one that was presently visible. Nobody else could see these figures and when she realized that fact, she blocked them out and says, 'I just stopped seeing them.'

Some mediums describe a similar genesis for their alleged psychic abilities and consider these ethereal forms not to be alien, or inter-dimensional, of course, but to be the spirits of the dead in some unknown afterlife whom they later commune with on a regular basis. On the other hand, at least one person who has seen these wraith-like forms (which, I am told, are just like ordinary people in appearance) regards them as living in our own future, somehow being witnessed across time.

Returning to Gwyneth, she also learnt to filter out these perceptions that others did not share, especially when her family told her she was too imaginative for her own good. But the same practice failed to remove all her weird experiences.

She found herself standing outside looking up at the stars 'with a terrible longing inside of me' and feeling a voice 'up there', whose words she could not take in, that was drawing her towards it like a magnet. She felt a part of space, not apart from it.

By her teenage years, following a series of out-of-body sensations, visions of an alien figure and various other strange events, she was taken on the round of doctors and diagnosed as suffering from temporal lobe epilepsy. As a result she was given rather barbaric shock treatment, allegedly to cure this physical impediment. It only succeeded in leaving her with countless intense migraines.

Again, there are various cases on record of star children suffering from severe migraines and Gwyneth is by no means the only one who was labelled epileptic as a consequence.

Epilepsy seems to be a medical option that appears to resolve the strange things these people report – odd feelings (which I would call the Oz Factor), voices out of nowhere (which are not considered normal, of course) and impossible visions (which are only impossible in our consensus view of reality). However, in few cases that I know about where such medical conclusions have been reached, has the treatment resulted in a better, healthier person. A magic wand is waved but does not rid them of their ESP.

After the shock treatment Gwyneth found that the periods of time lapse in her life got worse. The doctors felt these occurred when she briefly lost consciousness during an epileptic seizure. There is little doubt that many UFOlogists would have regressed her using hypnosis and tried to reveal memories of a hidden alien kidnap. It hardly matters who is right – medicine or UFOlogy. The only question that counts is whether either option would make Gwyneth, and others like her, feel better. I suspect that is very doubtful in cases such as this.

Gradually, Gwyneth incorporated her experiences into the philosophy of Spiritualism, to which she was introduced when a young woman. This helped find a niche for the disparate phenomena that were plaguing her existence and probably aided her more than anything up to that point. Indeed I suspect – without wishing to disparage Spiritualism (I have an open mind on the idea of life after death) – that many people who become mediums may, given just a slight nudge in a different direction, have instead become contactees or alien abductees. Some of the claims of famous medium Doris Collins, for example, imply this.

As Gwyneth grew older her experiences filled out into more well-channelled directions – vivid, lucid dreams, out-of-body sensations, etc. Then she frequently began to see and to dream about UFOs and aliens and this tended to direct her attention in a different way. Once she discovered the claims of abductees it was as if a picture had suddenly come into sharp focus. Not surprisingly she reinterpreted her time lapses, strange creatures and lights in the sky as possible evidence of alien intervention in her life. Then she recalled her wanderlust for the stars and pondered its meaning.

It is easy to assume that Gwyneth is a star child. But the nagging question that will not go away is whether to presume that possibility merely replaces one philosophy with another. If spirits of the dead can be scapegoats for a latent talent in us all – is the same not true of aliens?

David from Bristol is another example of this process in action. He was born in 1942, which in itself is interesting. According to American researcher Budd Hopkins, an extraordinary number of abductees were either born that year or began to have their experiences between 1942 and 1943. I have to say that I have noticed this trend also. The first two British abduction cases – one consciously recalled and one not – both happened in that year, which is, in fact, five years before the term 'flying saucer' was invented and when the UFO mystery thus officially came into being.

As a child David had countless vivid dreams, examples of poltergeist activity around his prefab home and would hear odd noises coming out of nowhere. Objects would move around rooms on their own. Lights would switch on and off. He also had 'impulses' to go to certain locations in the middle of town and stand and wait. Upon doing so people would meet him who had also been driven there in a similar manner.

David is another of those who spontaneously described his adventures with psychic toys. The balls of light would appear in his bedroom and dance around the room, play on the walls and then disappear.

In 1955, his experiences with UFOs began in earnest when he was delivering newspapers. As he wheeled his bicycle away from a house an object appeared out of nowhere over waste ground. It was a 'classic flying saucer shape' with a huge dome on top of a disc and a row of portholes on the edge pouring out brilliant light in blue and orange.

The object was so vivid, so spectacular and just simply hovering there at 5 p.m. as the rush hour commuter traffic flooded out of the city, that half of Bristol should have seen this thing. Of course, that did not occur. It appears that nobody other than David saw any of this dazzling display. It was as if it were a stage show that had been put on solely for his benefit.

As he watched the craft he was ensnared by the Oz Factor, time spread out like strawberry jam, a wonderful sense of peace and calm descended upon the young boy and there were no sounds of traffic or people – just a oneness between himself and infinity as represented by this visitor from somewhere beyond our comprehension.

This link between mind and miracle only broke when the thing disappeared. It did not fly away like a jumbo jet or zoom into orbit like a rocket ship, it melded into the sky and simply dematerialized. One second it was there, challenging reality, the next it had gone back to whence it came.

Finally, I must mention a case investigated by the late D. Scott Rogo, who was a clever man whose research we will all miss. This takes us one step further into real alien territory and also helps illustrate that Britain is but a pebble on the intergalactic beach. These phenomena happen everywhere.

Sammy Desmond was Hispanic and lived in Reseda in the San Fernando Valley near Los Angeles, California. Again, he began to have psychic experiences as a young child. By the age of six he was seeing a strange figure of a misty texture beside his bed and also had other episodes where feelings and sensations on the borderline of reality imposed into his sleep.

As a teenager Sammy endured violent poltergeist energies. Whilst helping out at his father's construction company, metal objects would bend and snap in his hands. If he placed a key in a door lock it would often warp and then break in two. It should be stressed that this was before Uri Geller arrived on the scene to dazzle the world with his alleged spoon-bending activities (although it might also be worth mentioning that Geller links his powers with an extraterrestrial intelligence that he believes he has communicated with for many years).

Sammy Desmond's experiences were always spontaneous. Unlike Geller's performances, he could never make them happen to order. Yet even thick beams of metal warped from time to time in his presence as if he were occasionally exuding a powerful aura.

You will not be surprised to hear that balls of light appeared in the Desmond household as well. As Rogo reports: '[they] typically consisted of a football-sized glowing and spinning object surrounded by similar but slightly smaller objects. Desmond reported the lights to other family members, who tended to dismiss the sightings, even though his youngest sister reported seeing them in her room.'

After frequent visits by these psychic toys, one of them descended towards Sammy and he became paralysed and lost consciousness. There is an indication of the Oz Factor being in effect (Desmond told Rogo his mind was in a 'weird mood' whenever the lights came into his room).

Eventually, after using what appears to have been mental communication or even psycho-kinesis to repel the lights away from him, the youth succumbed and let these balls have their way with him. The first time it happened six hours disappeared from his recall in an instant.

The culmination of these conscious experiences came one night when he heard dogs barking and horses kicking up a fuss at the back of the house and he went to the window to take a look. Sammy now saw several small entities scrambling towards a fence and then heading for the house. They wore one-piece suits and helmets with visors over their heads. He rushed to slam the back door of the house shut to stop them getting in, waking the family with the racket. The entities had by then completely disappeared.

It is interesting that when he took these stories (and various others we do not have space to discuss) to university parapsychologist Rogo, Sammy was very much disinclined to connect them with UFOs and rather perceived the creatures and lights as demonic in origin. Hypnosis did follow, via former UCLA psychologist Dr Thelma Moss, just before the appearance of Whitley Strieber's story in *Communion* and Budd Hopkins' publication of his research in *Intruders* in the spring of 1987. So we can at least be sure that Desmond was not compromised by any knowledge of those cases or the splurge of publicity that descended on America in their wake.

As a consequence of the hypnosis sessions a detailed story emerged about what supposedly has happened between Sammy and these alien entities over the course of time. We will return to this in chapter six when the finer points of this become particularly relevant.

The discovery in this chapter that victims of abduction have a lifelong history of supernatural phenomena clearly means something. We should add it to the clues already found about these people's visual creativity (artistic talents) and extraordinary recall of early life memories. Together they point us toward something special; perhaps about the brain or maybe the genetic make-up of the individual concerned. Either way it is the first real sign that there is something that marks such people out from the rest of humanity and may prime one to becoming a star child.

Those who see this as a negative factor are presuming that a psychological solution must by necessity apply. But that is not at all certain. If we find evidence that star children are different then there are two possibilities that come to mind.

They could be artistic, have strong memories and

experience oodles of supernatural things because they are hyper-imaginative and these are all by-products, just as is the slightly more bizarre experience of the alien abduction.

On the other hand, being a star child might leave its mark more explicitly, through physiology or parapsychology. In that respect, visual creativity, excellent recall of early life and psychic track records may be very real, merely symptoms of that actual difference.

In other words, if you are primed for ESP you are also primed for alien contact.

If there are two people standing side by side and one of them sees the sun in the sky whilst the other one perceives nothing but darkness, then it would be foolish to conclude that the sun does not exist, even on the seemingly sensible grounds that, if it did, then both of these people would surely have seen it.

Of course, there may be no such thing as the sun and the one who says there is may be deluded. Yet we must not forget that they may also be capable of seeing the sun when the other person – by reason of their own limitations – is not.

These assorted weird phenomena are real within the purview of these various witnesses. It is difficult to argue any other than that fact. Are we so sure of our own brand of truth that we must stand up and denounce these things as not 'really' being real? Or is that easy way out little better than an admission of defeat?

5 We Are Starlight ...

Christine made final preparations for lift-off. The countdown was well underway. Soon, very soon, the ship would rise towards the stars – climbing majestically from the launchpad in an effortless, silent arc.

Her brother stood grinning nearby, unconvinced by the performance and only mildly wrapped up in the transient joy of the game.

This was not Apollo 11 and the launchpad was no Cape Canaveral. There was no rocket fuel dripping from the tanks, just some old magnets held onto the bottom. The ship would rise from a little back-yard high above the terraced streets of Rusholme, Manchester, passing the floodlit pylons of nearby Maine Road soccer stadium and travelling onward toward infinity.

The spacecraft itself was hardly a multi-million-dollar construction. It was an ordinary household dustbin.

Christine counted down, ' ... 3 – 2 – 1', with the tension not exactly mounting.

But then something happened. Something impossible. The small metal module wobbled ever so slightly on its gantry of crumbling bricks that had recently been extracted from the war-time Anderson shelter now acting as a household coal store.

It was a small motion at first, then slightly bigger. Then, almost as if it had a bout of hiccups, the dustbin jerked into the air and nestled back down onto the bricks again.

The rise had been minute – inches at most. But it *seemed* real. It *had been* real. This concoction of everyday objects had made it briefly into space at an overall cost of less than five pounds.

Christine was shocked. The event was mind-numbing in its simplicity, yet profound in all its consequences. She turned to her brother to ask if he had seen it too. He was already looking away, bored, seeking something else to play with. Christine resolved never to try this trick again.

This tale is as true as I can remember it. It did take place when I was young. That is, I had the vision that this dustbin had briefly risen into the air. Whether it actually did rise is probably another matter.

At the time I had experienced my first few strange episodes with lights and noises. I was also beginning to have fits of ESP.

My maternal grandmother had, perhaps innocently, encouraged these. Indeed she was very psychic herself. We had no telephone and nor did she. But whenever I, or my brother, or my parents were ill she would just turn up on the doorstep having made the twenty-mile Ribble bus ride from Bacup to be with us. I can see her now, standing at the door, announcing without a moment's hesitation or hint of mystification: 'I had to come. I knew that sommat was up.'

Armed with this support I did not shut out strange happenings, such as vivid dreams that seemed to be significant. I listened to them, collected and studied them, then pondered their meaning.

In one dream I saw an aircraft crash from the sky into the streets of a strange town. I was unsure where it was but noticed the unusual red and cream buses, and wrote that into my note-book. The next day the family went home to Rossendale for the weekend and on the Sunday the news broke about an aircraft that had fallen onto the centre of Stockport as it approached Manchester Airport. Some weeks later we visited this town on a shopping trip. The buses were red and cream, just as I had seen them in my dream.

Of course, during the mid-sixties real journeys into outer space were on the minds of many children as the billion-dollar yearning to reach the moon took shape. No doubt others played games rather like I did.

Yet this backyard spaceship was not just a game. It was more than that. I do not know why it was different, but it was. Although I realize that there was no way that dustbin can have really flown, it was an experiment that cried out to be done. It fulfilled a purpose in my life. And it left me satisfied afterwards in some curious fashion.

I bought a large telescope with money from my newspaper delivery round and battled against the sodium street-lamps to peer outward into the universe. The six-inch reflector was heavy and I could not lift it on my own. But until others tired of the ritual of carrying it onto the small croft near the front of our house I made the most of it.

The moons of Jupiter, the Andromeda nebula and the phases of Venus all became visible against the orange hue of bustling nocturnal city life.

I was enraptured by all of this, utterly captivated by the sense of endless space and the riddle of time that the universe provided. Yet there was more to it than that, a subtlety behind the fascination. It was as if I was trying to find something lost up there within the stars.

Crosby, Stills, Nash and Young said it in their song *Woodstock*, which at this unique point in history symbolized a mood abroad within the world. They spoke of how a universal desire to return to some imperceptible source was washing through humanity – perhaps an image of Eden serving as a metaphor for this vanished paradise. They said to the youth culture of the day: 'We are starlight ... we are golden ... We have to get back to the garden ...' And that is a feeling star children seem to know all too well.

After some years of braving the stares of gangs of youths and the unwelcome attention of one or two rough and ready teenage boys, I abandoned these expeditions with the telescope further than our back-yard. But I was already familiar with the layout of the cosmos and consuming avidly books that delved into the important questions that nagged persistently at me.

Were we alone in all this vastness? Could there be other life-forms out there waiting for us? Did they ever come to visit us – and, if so, what did they hope to find here? It was in this that I discovered UFOs.

*   *   *

Of course, you are perfectly entitled – indeed no doubt
more than likely – to see nothing strange in any of this. A
childhood interest piqued by the NASA moonshots –
active imagination, natural curiosity – just what is weird
about any of that?

Probably nothing. For many years I saw nothing odd
about it either. But I was often asked later what got me
interested in UFOs. What led eventually to my life
changing so drastically that I was consumed by a
seemingly pointless quest to answer its apparently trivial
questions.

The peculiar thing is that when I was asked, by other
UFOlogists, those who attended my lectures or from time
to time in media interviews, I buried these childhood
memories in my mind and guarded them like a jealous
secret. I knew they were there. I just would not talk about
them.

In fact, I would always say that I became interested in
UFOs because I trained to teach science and was intrigued
by questions on the borderline of knowledge. That is not
really untrue. But it sidesteps the issue. There has to be
something more that turns a healthy interest into a driving
obsession. I would never discuss the London light, the
Blackpool UFO, the piece of the sky that fell upon the
Rossendale hills, or, most of all, this moment in time when
a dustbin defied the known laws of the universe.

Then, many years later, in the mid 1980s, I met a young
man from Oldham. We'll call him Don.

He was a fascinating chap in his late teens. He had a
look about him which made you think he was staring
vacantly past you, or indeed past the whole world and out
into some distant void. He would often stay silent for long
periods and then suddenly proffer the most bizarre
comment or profound statement. Then he would clam up
again for the rest of the night.

One day, Don had called me and asked if I would meet
him somewhere for a talk. We agreed upon a cafe in the
centre of Manchester and I came prepared to hear what he

had to say for half an hour or so. In fact we stayed most of the afternoon, lurking at a corner table, the catering staff eyeing us suspiciously as we consumed the occasional cup of coffee.

Don had a story to tell that was far beyond my expectations, especially as I had known him then for a couple of years and not suspected any of this.

He told me how from the age of five or six his life had been plagued with odd experiences. As these tumbled out I began to realize just how familiar many of them were.

Don had seen UFOs – which, given his home was in the Pennines, was not a particular surprise to me. But, he added, there followed a very bizarre experience where something had saved his life.

He had been playing in an old building with some other boys and rather foolishly clambered over the roof. Suddenly this gave way and he crashed through it. Below him loomed concrete and certain death. There was no way he could survive the large drop. As he fell he felt time slow down and his life unwind. Then it was as if he was gripped by unseen hands and placed gently onto the floor. He hit the ground, shook himself a little and essentially walked away. His escape was near miraculous, but he felt it was not by chance that it had occurred.

After that two odd things began to dominate his life. He would have an undefined feeling to go to certain places – perhaps the library steps – and stand there waiting. The urge was overwhelming, but he fought it off at first. When he succumbed he found himself meeting strange, blond-haired people who walked down the street and stared knowingly at him, appearing to convey information into his mind. It stayed there, locked away, tantalizingly out of reach and yet securely in place. Somehow, Don knew, it meant something.

Then he started to do experiments using magnets and electro-magnetic fields. He built them into circles, or rings, and wired these up to the mains. He spent day after day at this exercise convinced that somehow he was designing something important. The thing hummed, lights flickered. He had minor successes, but the goal that he was chasing eluded him. He knew that using these magnets he could make a free-standing circular object rise from the ground. It could levitate, drift away, defy gravity. It flew like a UFO.

Don could see that I was amazed, but mistook my glazed expression for disbelief. He did not know – indeed, nobody knew – about my experiment with the circular dustbin. Yet the vague urge that I had felt back then was exactly the same – if not taken to the same extreme or boosted with the same knowledge of electro-magnetism that Don had apparently possessed.

Seeking to convince me, Don brought out his notebooks and scrapbooks. These included a local newspaper cutting illustrating one of his sightings – others also referring to relevant incidents. There were photographs of his experiments too. Whatever else was true, Don really had built these circular magnets. He was perfectly sincere about that.

I owed him the news about my own little run-in with alien science, if only to demonstrate that I was not going to laugh or breach his confidence. I left that day convinced that this was something terribly important, but I did not know how or why. I suspected that in the shadows of the UFO underworld there were many other closet contactees deftly experimenting but never daring to speak about their foolish attempts at alien meccano. No doubt they were as concerned as I was about looking a complete idiot for spouting such evident nonsense in public.

I recalled many other things in the days after Don's confession.

I thought about the meeting that the alien, Gary, had asked Peter Warrington and I to set up for him with a respected scientist in London. That man had been working with electro-magnetism and had designed a revolutionary propulsion system. As we sat in his office in April 1976 he had demonstrated his experiments on a small-scale rotating model, delighting at how the object had seemed to defy gravity.

His experiments, remember, had involved alleged alien intervention even before we paid him a visit. In 1976 that had seemed utterly ridiculous to a naive, hard-headed and determinedly objective UFOlogist. When Peter and I wrote a brief account of this session into what was my first book (*UFOs: A British Viewpoint*, 1979) it was hard to mask that disbelief. Even the scientist had warned us never to mention his name and we had to promise to keep the tape recording of that day's meeting under lock and key until he was ready to go public for himself. He has yet to do so; although I have seen him in the media often. But we still have the tape and the letters exchanged with his university department to prove this did all happen.

From time to time others have written to me to tell me of their experiments to design alien propulsion systems. They usually involve rotating electro-magnets. If this is all just a delusion, then it seems remarkably widespread. Yet, superficially, the actual science behind the delusion appears to be absurd. That was one reason why the London professor was struggling for peer support and financial backing.

I also recalled the first time I met Tim Good, noted UFO writer and committed believer in the alien hypothesis. Whilst publicly I have rejected many of his theories, I have always respected his obvious sincerity. I also suspect that some of my rejection was based upon my inner rebellion. I was tearing myself away from his conclusions with a subconscious vengeance.

Tim had often spoken of how he, and others, had met strange blond-haired people in mundane places, such as hotel lobbies, and received curious, knowing smiles from them and what amounted to a telepathic rapport. It was part of a philosophical substrata of UFOlogy that there were aliens living on earth in human guise. I had never taken it seriously. It seemed ridiculous.

More recently Oscar-winning actress and neo-mystic Shirley MacLaine had said much the same thing in a series of books relating her exploration into UFO phenomena, which had seen her spend time with contactees and 'star children'. Some of this was dramatized in the TV mini-series *Out on a Limb*, in which she played herself seeking the alien meaning of life.

All of this was simmering beneath the surface for a while, but then the real firebomb burst in front of me in the form of a book called *Communion* penned by horror novelist Whitley Strieber.

I got a copy from the USA in early 1987, some months before it reached the UK, possibly because Strieber credits the writings of Peter Warrington and myself, which he chanced to read one Christmas and which first alerted him to the link between curious memories and the alien contact mystery. Strieber's expertly written and powerful story of his own quest for understanding became a global best-seller, retailing millions of copies and exerting more influence than any other book in the history of the UFO subject. It inspired a movie, starring Christopher Walken as the novelist.

Whatever anyone thinks about Strieber's story – and he had an uneasy relationship with UFOlogists and (it must be said) a less than straightforward rapport with me – one thing cannot be denied. Strieber's story reaches out and shakes you to the core, filled as it is with well-told insights and parallels. He speaks of things that so few people know, even within the complex field of UFO enthusiasm.

Notably, his pages 116 and 117 hit me (and Don) like a bulldozer with the brakes off. Strieber tells, as a simple anecdote, how at the age of thirteen he told a friend that spacemen had shown him how to build a machine to defy gravity. He then set up an assemblage of electro-magnets, wired it to the mains at his childhood home in Texas and watched as it whirred into life and caused the house lights to glow and then explode. Later a fire burnt the roof above this spot and he stopped his impromptu experimentation.

There is clearly no possibility that Strieber knew of Don's story when he wrote this, or that Don knew his when he did his own experiments. Yet they are so similar to one another that there seems little alternative to them both being true. Indeed, Strieber adds that he has since discovered others in the UFO field who have had similar dealings with alien technology – as had I.

Some words from a CIA document may be apposite here. Ironically this was dated April 1976, the same month that we took Gary and his story to the electrical engineer in London. It was released later under the Freedom of Information Act which is now law in the USA.

The CIA describe how, despite the official closure of US government interest in UFOs during 1969, they are still 'monitoring UFO reporting channels' and that data is being compiled by scientific staff whose calibre is such that it removes them from the 'nut' category (!). Moreover, that a principal aim of this research is connected with something that the released memos have never expanded upon, but which is described succinctly as 'UFO propulsion systems'.

So it seems even the CIA regard this as the hub of the UFO mystery.

Up until now we have only looked at people being rescued by unknown entities, strange compulsions to build weird machinery, unusual anecdotes that pop up in somebody's life and a vague sort of thread that links these all together. This is odd enough. But we could just envisage a kind of alien mentor attempting to spread the word through all of these people. We may even argue that it might be a whole lot simpler just to leave one of these antigravity machines on the lawns of Cambridge University or MIT!

However, when we probe deeper into cases where the witness slots these various things together into an all-embracing concept a new, worrying thought emerges. This sees these people not as having a mere hotline to alien technology, but rather as being aliens in their own right. That, yes, extraterrestrials are living here on earth. These folk are them!

We have mentioned Gary a few times so far, and he was my first direct contact with someone professing to be not of this earth. He broached this subject cautiously, first referring to himself as a 'representative of the aliens'. By the end of a year he was professing to be an extraterrestrial spirit that had reincarnated into several earth bodies in the past. He saw life on earth as a penance, but as an important task also. He had to get his message across and took every opportunity to drill facts and figures into me and to reach out to anybody else who would listen to him. He remains active through other people now. Yet he does not seek any publicity or self-glory for his work. His is a very lonely crusade.

To be honest neither Peter Warrington nor I were particularly impressed by Gary's rambling stories about Nostradamus and his prophecies. Those quatrains which were written in the sixteenth century can be read many ways to try to predict the future, often unsuccessfully; although this was the first time I had come across an alien attempting to manipulate them to spell out what amounted to a business card introducing himself!

Gary told us that as a child in Northamptonshire he recalled a moment when, in the garden, he was surrounded by light pouring down from above. Overhead was a strange craft and he felt a terrible sense of loss and desertion as it departed. He interpreted this as being dumped on earth by his alien colleagues, his spirit imprisoned in the body of an earth boy.

At that point I had not met any witnesses who claimed to have had alien contact. In 1975 there simply were none of them in Britain. Much later, having talked to perhaps one hundred or more such people, I came to see that the sense of loss on the departure of the UFO was a very common reaction. 'It was like I had just said goodbye to my dearest friend,' one witness told me. Another, a hard-headed woman who coped with the trials and tribulations of running a home that boarded wayward children, reported how she burst into tears as the UFO flew away. 'I wept inconsolably,' she described.

The ending of the encounter – far from being a joyful relief – was, strangely, often sorrowful. Indeed, aliens usually promise the witnesses that they will return in the future as one way of making them feel better, when, in truth, you might expect the best news that these aliens could offer would be, 'Don't worry, this is the last you'll ever see of us.'

In retrospect I thought for a long time that Gary may have simply experienced this common (if baffling) emotional abreaction – a kind of post-abduction blues – and read into it things that were not there, such as his desertion by the beings from the UFO. But then again Jayne, the Manchester nurse, had, if you recall, felt the same sadness in her vision of an alien homeland. And many of the children who described having played with psychic toys in their bedrooms had been tearful when these went away. This theme of separation from a place where one belongs does seem to be an important, if rather unexpected, feature of the alien contact story.

However unconvincing Gary's shuffling of Nostradamus anecdotes might have been, he did promise Peter and I that he would provide 'sugar' (his word) if we arranged the contact with the scientist whom he wanted to meet. That meeting took place, as you have heard, in April 1976. Within six months we were suddenly swamped with a wave of alien contact cases – so much so that 1976 is still known as Britain's 'year of the humanoids'.

In one case, from Leeds, an ambulance driver met aliens who gave him a truly odd message – saying something about the 'Alpha and Omega' and how '100 years are but a day to us'. Days before, almost as if he had set it all up (although I have no evidence to suspect that he did), Gary had told me nearly word for word this exact same thing over the phone.

As if that were not explicit enough, a woman called Joyce Bowles and a man called Ted Pratt had what became the first well-publicized alien abduction in Britain when they say their car was stalled by a being that got out of a landed craft on a by-pass near Winchester. This was in November. When I first saw the drawing that these witnesses made of their alien captor I stared at it and then burst out laughing. It was (and still is) highly unusual to claim to have met bearded aliens. But that is what they saw – moreover, their sketch was like a police identikit picture of Gary.

It was hard to experience such things and emerge completely unscathed, faithfully proclaiming nothing but the laws of chance and coincidence.

Since then I have been contacted by many others whose views about their own alien origin are either more or less specific than Gary's. They use all kinds of devices to express themselves. They may write anonymously – they may phrase themselves humorously, then apologize – or they may just couch all they say in terms like, 'I know you won't believe it – I hardly can believe it for myself ... but ...' The theme that links them all together is obvious.

Audrey from Devon wrote to explain how it started for her. A simple, fairly straightforward UFO sighting in October 1971 when she lived in Essex. Other people saw it too. There was no doubting its reality. But, as so often is the case, it was the aftermath that was more significant.

As she said; 'I felt compelled to write a short story. [It] poured out as if dictated to me.' The story was all about an alien mission to earth – in effect the lowdown on what the UFO subject was all about.

Then she had a vivid, lucid dream, in which she knew that she was dreaming and could affect its outcome. In this she was staring at strange symbols on a wall and called out for their meaning. They faded and were replaced by a tall, shimmering alien entity who 'powered' images into her brain.

After this she felt a terrible urge to write to an author and tell him some seemingly ridiculous things, a correspondence that continued as Audrey began to churn out more automatic writing offering weird tales about the meaning of UFOlogy. These were reputedly being dictated to her by the alien who called himself 'Gok'. The author took this in good part and told her that he had reached similar conclusions himself. Both he and Audrey had found that they were pawns in a kind of grand alien plan of enlightenment.

I have been told this too, once, by a government source and was given the name 'the education programme' for the long-term process. The idea is that bits and pieces of the truth are being planted into the subconscious of many people, who will one day be stirred into action. They are seeds that germinate all over the world hoisting mankind towards a new understanding. Often these people do not realize that they are any part of this. But one day the whole thing will slot into place like a giant jigsaw puzzle.

However, Audrey was then told something more worrying. She was not just a pawn. Both she and her writer friend had known one another in a previous lifetime when they had both lived as other people on a planet in a star system of alpha centauri. Not surprisingly, this was too much for the author. He could not accept that part of the story at all.

Audrey's correspondence with Gok went on for years and she was fed a whole host of material about the alien plan on earth. But, as she says, how can one tell if this is real or just her own subconscious in overdrive?

Another frustrated star child to contact me (with a postcode that indicated she was from the Midwest of the USA) pleaded for help, saying that she did not know where she was or why she could remember all of this.

In November 1979 she was abducted and told by 'my people' that she was one of them. They showed her Australia and Miami, Florida, which were strong focal points of alien presence.

The rest of her letter was hard to translate, discussing as it did a sense of imprisonment on earth, a desire to return home but a feeling that there was a task to perform which would prevent that for the present. She also added that the Ogalala Sioux Indians and the Aboriginal peoples were somehow more aware of what was happening and that their legends spoke of this.

Quite the strangest correspondence I have received from a self-professed star child was from a woman in Edinburgh who was either possessed of a vivid imagination or near total recall of what had happened to her.

She claimed that the aliens in control were from a planet orbiting the star zeta tucanae in the reticula system (an origin frequently suggested in contactee lore). They could interbreed with humans, although they themselves were white-skinned with Oriental eyes and hairless bodies.

These creatures had been visiting her home at night for years, but blocking the memory, which largely only emerged as dreams. She knew that she was 'different' from others as a result of all this, but not why.

This began in 1959 when as a child she awoke to find herself standing in the hall in the middle of the night, light pouring through a wall vent. She was confused and unable to understand what she was doing standing there. Then a long silver tube with a red light on the end was pushed through the letter-box of the flats and she lost consciousness.

That was just the first of many similar episodes. In January 1979, along with her parents, she saw a UFO hovering over the city sports stadium, and reported this to a UFO group, BUFORA. It marked the genesis of her conscious recall – pieced together in subsequent months by a series of dreams, which she carefully remembered and then analysed. From these she could work out more and more about her frequent visits to see 'them', making sense at last of why she would habitually stand by the window at night staring into space. She had done this odd thing since a child.

She knows how others will react. When she first began to understand she was 'just as surprised and sceptical as you are now'. However, she likens the memory to having two minds – part of which knows what day of the week it is, the other being locked in another time and space.

If what she says is to be believed the earth is like a giant transit lounge where entities from various worlds go about their business – sometimes as themselves (i.e. in their own bodies), sometimes by inhabiting earth bodies in a form of spirit possession (as with herself) but also by a programme of genetic interbreeding that at least one of the groups of alien visitors performs. This results in alien/human hybrids walking the earth. They seem normal, but star children can tell them apart from ordinary people. These are presumably the ones often referred to as the blond-haired, blue-eyed and smiling spiritual entities that commune with selected witnesses in a telepathic fashion and plant information into their heads and strange urges to go to places and do certain things.

Of course, I am not suggesting that any of these claims are literally true, merely using them to reflect the extent of this belief and the widespread nature of its themes, notably reference to an experimental programme. Bear in mind the relative lack of public knowledge about star child theories.

One writer apologized profusely for describing the

aliens as if he were one of them – 'It's crazy, I know, but it's a lot easier for me this way.'

He explained how he (as an alien) was not alone and

we are here for a reason of survival. Your kind belong to us ... we have existed long before your time hence our technological superiority ... we can manipulate time/space contortions ... [but] we can no longer reproduce ourselves ... to overcome this we had to perform an experiment ... this had to be done for our survival. We are not malevolent by nature, but others may be ...

More information was offered about this genetic experiment. Both human males and females are used – male sperm being taken and then altered using alien genes. 'This is then inserted to cause impregnation of your female. The resulting foetus is then removed and kept for the purpose of continuous hybrid technology which will be completed [soon].'

As you see, this genetic experiment is reputedly of great importance to what is happening so we shall turn to that now for further investigation.

6 Spacenapped

Steve Andrews from Cardiff, South Wales, has a spaceship. He built it himself. But it does not fly. Instead, he plays music with it!

Steve is typical of those gifted and visually creative people who may well be candidates for star children. Expressing his talents through singing/songwriting, he conjures up flowing lyrics that are more akin to poetry. Others of his ilk create similar effects, with or without music. Steve has often credited his 'spaceship' on album jackets and it features on several tracks.

Steve Andrews is also not afraid to talk about his extensive experiences and resultant philosophy regarding UFOs and alien contact. He has written to me of the orange balls of light, the strange figures in his bedroom at night and, most interesting of all, his alien mentor who appears to him in vivid dreams. This is a female entity entitled 'Philateloos'.

Female aliens do occur in quite a few cases. Whilst they are very common with male abductees they are reported not infrequently by women as well.

Steve Andrews' memories (or dreams) about his alien friend do not extend beyond the realms of an amiable tutor or guide. Indeed this rapport is so great that in some cases like this it can border on the angelic guardian that some witnesses we met earlier have described.

American researcher Brad Steiger has collected a number of cases of a similar nature.

He tells how Tom, a movie producer from Florida, almost drowned as a child at the age of four whilst playing in the seas off New Jersey. As he sank, swallowing water and knowing that death was imminent, he went out of his body and met a figure he calls his 'guardian' who advised Tom to return to earth. Reputedly, he was living during the present time period for a specific, pre-arranged, reason. He was eventually given the option to 'die' or 'continue your mission' and agreed to do the latter.

Bobby from North Carolina ran into the path of a truck in 1968 when he was five years old. He then suffered the Oz Factor, with time slowing to a crawl and his consciousness switching into another level of reality. A strange entity with dark blond hair materialized at his side and whisked him from under the wheels of the vehicle as they were rapidly bearing down on him. Bobby was rolled toward the curb, hearing his mother's cries. The strange being was no longer in sight. But fourteen years later he encountered a UFO whilst on holiday in Wisconsin and immediately recalled the being that he had seen as a child. The same emotional bond was reawakened by the sighting.

Then there is Michael from Seattle, Washington, who was also five when he saw a light-haired, tall being with blue eyes as he played in some woods. The being spoke telepathically and called him 'son', which mystified Michael. Indeed he actually spoke out in reply: 'You are not my father.' But he has seen this man often since in dreams. The being seems to watch over Michael's life, as if protecting him and warning of the right path to take.

Taking cases like these together you can see that there is a strong database of witnesses who believe they are somehow related or in tune with superior entities. Those beings are aware of a much deeper plan behind the everyday trivialities of life. In the past such reports would undoubtedly have been interpreted as interventions by God, and that kind of evaluation will still be preferred by some today. Others will, no doubt, regard these figures as spiritual ones, perhaps wise beings in an afterlife. But, at least as often, the witnesses themselves view them as alien – some kind of superior intelligence from somewhere else that has placed them on earth to engage in a plan that appears crucial to this point in history but of which the star children themselves have no apparent conscious recall.

Many of these cases are not what we would call abductions. There is contact between the humans and these wise alien entities but it occurs *ad hoc* throughout life and is a bit like meeting up with a long-lost uncle on a rare visit from some distant country. Indeed these stories have more than a passing resemblance to the so-called contactees of the 1950s, which many UFOlogists derided at the time. These contactees (they were mostly men) would claim to have had friendly chats with alien pals who wanted them to make the world a better place. As a result various groups and cults were launched.

However, cases like the 1950s contactees, or the more modern angelic guardians, offer a striking contrast to the non-voluntary, far from friendly and usually repellent alien abductions of recent times. People (and there are at least at many women as men in such cases) are being kidnapped by these aliens, medically experimented upon and then dumped back home with precious little memory of what has taken place. Any memory that does bubble up from the surface usually comes much later, often through dreams or artificial means such as regression hypnosis – thus seeming to challenge its authenticity in many responsible researchers' eyes.

The question is, are these really two separate phenomena or are they both manifestations of the same mystery? Ought we not to look more closely at the idea that contactees are just examples of such so-called spacenappings, where the one-to-one relationship has never consciously extended to any medical experimentation?

We may have to take this option seriously, because of the way in which the two phenomena have a worrying tendency to overlap.

You have already seen how some neo-contactees are being told that part of the alien plan involves genetic experiments to place human/alien hybrid babies here on earth. The aliens are, in effect, seeking to justify their medical practices as reported so frequently in the more drastic modern cases.

Equally, abductees commonly report characteristics that

are most often found in the contactee stories. They tell of the sense of deep emotional bonding with the entities and the idea of a long-term plan that they are not meant to know consciously about. Also they frequently cite the claim that the aliens have been in regular communication with their human captive since that person's childhood – exactly as, in fact, do many contactees.

Here are just a few quotes from abductees talking about such matters. You will quickly appreciate that they are difficult to distinguish from the statements made elsewhere in this book coming from what are, in effect, contactees. Remember that all of the witnesses cited in the next few paragraphs are victims of full-blown modern spacenappings complete with medical experimentation – the abductees that form the basis of huge current attention in supposedly scientific research. They are not at all what most researchers would regard as contactees.

'He knows me from before. But how does he know me?' (Witness spacenapped in New York state, USA, May 1968.)

'You are our children. You are part of an experiment. We have been watching you constantly. Information and tasks to perform have been given to you. When the time is right you will know what they are.' (One of a family of five abducted in Essex in October 1974.)

'They are putting information into my head like hundreds and thousands ... When the time is right I will remember it. I haven't been told yet when to remember ... [They say] it will be during and after the sequence of events.' (A witness spacenapped in Lancashire in January 1976.)

'[He] knows me? ... 'How do you know?' ... 'I dunno ... He just told me.' ... 'What does he say exactly?' ... He says, 'Don't you remember me? ...' (part of a conversation under hypnosis between a West Yorkshire policeman and a doctor following the police officer's November 1980 encounter).

'I was told that I was chosen because I have a "cosmic mind". They have used a machine to plant a message that I will never forget.' (Man abducted in Brazil in December 1983.)

In his 1987 book Whitley Strieber frequently illustrates the same pattern. On page 261 he recounts a debate between himself and several victims of spacenapping who, in 1986, openly discussed their memories and feelings. The one thing they most strongly agreed upon is that there is a process of 'continuous monitoring' in which the entities keep tabs on their victims throughout life.

'We are participating willingly in this ongoing experience. They hope to build to the point where these beings can interact with us consciously and we will not be traumatized.' (One of the men who has been investigated by Harvard psychologist Dr John Mack, describing his spacenapping in Massachusetts in June 1992.)

A far more intimate interaction between the female alien and male human has also long been reported during examples of 'spacenapping'. Together they form what reads like an X-rated story. We cannot know whether this is a physical reality or just a psychological truth, but the way these stories all slot together into a startling pattern can only be disturbing to anyone who bothers to study the evidence.

We can start simply with a report from Barry,* a man from the Midlands, who despite obvious acute embarrassment told me what happened to him after seeing me appear alongside an abductee on national television.

Barry was with his girlfriend in her car in summer 1979. Both were teenagers and they had driven out onto Cannock Chase, Staffordshire, to visit a country pub. Suddenly, they heard strange noises inside the car that persisted for just a couple of seconds. They debated whether the radio had been accidentally switched on, decided it had not and left it at that. But then they realized that something else had taken place.

The car was now almost sucked dry of air. They had to wind down the windows in order to breathe. Then the same sounds as before filled the car, there was a whooshing noise and a red glowing light streaked towards the front of the vehicle as if from directly overhead. It hovered there briefly and sped off at a terrific rate over the hedgerows.

His girlfriend was shaking her head, partly in disbelief and partly in excitement saying, 'I've seen one.' Barry, ever the pragmatist, was telling her not to get carried away. There could be an explanation – even though he could not think of one that made much sense.

Eventually they carried on to his girlfriend's home, expecting it to be about 11.30 p.m. In fact it was 12.20 a.m. He had a lot of explaining to do to her parents, but did not use the UFO story as an excuse.

A while later, when Barry reached home and got undressed he noticed that his underpants were soiled and that his penis showed evidence of having ejaculated. He swears that he had not engaged in anything sexually arousing that evening. Yet, curiously, his girlfriend immediately showed signs of a pregnancy (her periods were disrupted for several weeks). They were very puzzled and concerned, but when she mustered the courage to have a pregnancy test everything was normal.

Some years later, when Barry first saw a copy of Strieber's book *Communion* on a bookshelf, he froze in panic. As he says, when reporting this for the first time, 'I'm not for one moment saying we were abducted, it was an alien craft or I recognize their faces ... I just feel as if I do recognize them ... Every word I have written is the truth and still I feel as if I am being silly.'

I feel sure Barry is being sincere and he has no need to have made up such a story to hide sexual transgressions (a theory one psychologist has espoused for a similar case). The tale he tells is clearly more damaging to his self-esteem than to simply admit he had fun with a girlfriend.

Of course, you will not need two guesses to work out what would almost certainly emerge were Barry (or his girlfriend) to be hypnotically regressed. If this story had been reported in the USA that would have happened soon after the tale was first told. As it was, the choice was left up to Barry and, perhaps glad to have got it off his chest and not wishing any further embarrassment, that appears to be as far as he wanted to take it.

Rather more complex memories are offered by 18-year-old Michael who was with his family in a country house in Zimbabwe. This was in July 1986.

He first encountered a bright flash of light that illuminated the road ahead, then hid behind bushes as an object like two pie plates on top of one another and ringed by windows swooped down and hovered directly over the spot that he had just vacated.

A few days later the same object materialized out of nowhere above his garden as he stood inexplicably staring into the sky. He dragged his parents out but by the time they arrived the object had gone.

Then on a third occasion he saw it in the presence of two others (his cousin and uncle). It disappeared by vanishing instantaneously on the spot.

During all of these encounters Michael felt as if he was watching in a detached manner – almost as if he were out of his body looking on – perhaps an important clue about the nature of these contacts. He also started to hear voices saying words in an unintelligible language inside his head.

In October that year Michael came to London and began to experience terrible nightmares and then to see strange figures in his bedroom in the middle of the night.

At first he called these beings 'ghosts' when talking to his parents. Then he used the name 'smurfs', after the comic-book characters. They only vaguely resembled these cartoon creations (i.e. three feet tall and surrounded by a blue glow). He noted that his reactions towards them and the light that filled the room were odd. Rather than respond as expected – yell out, call the police, etc. – it was as if he were under some sort of spell.

These beings had the ability to walk through doors as if they were not there and, in his best-recalled episode, had two taller entities with them. These beings were twice the size of the 'smurfs' and much more like human beings in appearance; although they wore what seemed to be doctors' gowns and acted as if prepared for an operation.

Then one entity spoke (mind to mind) saying, 'Don't you know me?' (more or less exactly what the Yorkshire police officer says the tall, gowned entity had spoken to him during his abduction). Without understanding why Michael had nodded in the affirmative and then he lost consciousness.

He came to on the floor with one of the tall entities extracting blood from both his index fingers. They also kept using a rod with a glass ball on the end to touch his body. This hurt when they did so, but despite his protests they carried on with the tactic. Then he lost consciousness again and awoke, still on the floor, with dawn breaking. He was totally disorientated but remembered the snatches of the experience as just described. But he felt too afraid to talk to anyone else about it.

Later that day Michael's lips and forehead began to swell painfully and it became so bad that a planned holiday was curtailed. He was taken to hospital by his mother. The doctors diagnosed an allergy of some sort, but he said nothing about the encounter in his bedroom.

As time went by Michael still had experiences with these strange visitors and became deeply withdrawn. He reached the point where he believed that he was going mad and went the rounds of various doctors and psychiatrists. Temporal lobe epilepsy was suggested (not the first time we have heard of a spacenap victim so diagnosed). Eventually, when he decided to bite the bullet and report these various alien contacts to his current psychiatrist the doctor then changed his conclusion to schizophrenia.

Michael strikes me as anything but mentally ill. As he sardonically noted, after working out his next step, 'I stopped talking about [these alien] visits and my doctor now says I am getting much better.'

In his most recently reported encounter, in spring 1993, Michael explains how he was awoken by a movement in his bedroom, then saw one of the grey beings and a lift or elevator shaft that suddenly materialized in the midst of the carpet. Inside this was one of the taller entities, gesturing to him to get out of bed and come inside the blue glow. He felt unable to resist and did so, then was sucked upwards through the ceiling as if it were not there at all and he was watching as the earth below receded.

Evidently, Michael had a deeper-level experience after this but the time is not yet right to make the details of this public. That is a very common statement from an abductee. I have heard it often.

Michael's thoughts about the meaning of all these experiences are very sophisticated. He adds that he is 'not sure if they come from outer space – they act more as if they come from this earth; their movements, their speech. I don't think anyone from another planet could master the English language.'

He has fascinating alternative ideas, likening aliens to 'bad fairies' in their activities and also noting: 'none of this may be happening. The UFOs, yes, I think they are definitely here. But the aliens? Witnesses could be exposed to radiation like microwaves which could cause a global psychosis with symptoms including seeing crea-tures, hearing voices and having abstract happenings.'

Does this sound like someone desperate for alien contact and wistfully creating a lifelong series of psychologically meaningful adventures?

We can also return to Scott Rogo's case of Sammy Desmond, from the San Fernando valley of California. We first met him in chapter four. This man's recollection, both conscious and under later hypnosis by Dr Thelma Moss, tells us a good deal about what he believes to have occurred when he was spacenapped by the small entities.

Indeed, so sexually explicit were some of the details that he was unable to talk openly about them to Dr Moss, becuse she was a woman. So, Rogo proceeded with future hypnosis sessions himself.

Desmond had a graphic image of the small beings displaying excessive interest in his genitals and of being shown strange scenes of himself lying naked. It was as if his emotional responses were being tested.

Physically, the examination consisted of clamps being placed around his body and a metal bar-like object being moved over his chest. Then a long pointed syringe was inserted into his abdomen. This was much longer than a hypodermic, being over two feet in size. Sammy felt pressure in his stomach but no pain. Some kind of dark liquid was in the end of the needle and this was apparently then injected into him.

David Jacobs, a history professor at Temple University in the USA, has made a special study of the details offered by abductees about the medical experiments that they claim to undergo. Several hundred such cases are now on record from around the world, although the majority are from the USA.

Indeed, three quarters of American abduction cases involve accounts of medical procedures but only one-third of British spacenappings do so. Most American researchers believe this to be because of the relative lack of hypnotic regression employed in Britain. The medical procedures are usually the most deeply buried memories and commonly need to be freed from the subconscious by rigorous artificial stimulation.

Jacobs reports that there is considerable touching involved in the examinations (e.g. the feeling of vertebrae). But the aliens never utilize standard procedures found in the routine medical tests of earthly doctors. No aliens ever take blood pressure or use stethoscopes to check heartbeats, for instance. If these stories were just fantasies, then some evidence of these mundane procedures ought to be expected, Jacobs argues.

The entities also seem particularly interested by any anomalies – e.g. if the witness wears contact lenses or false teeth.

However, the most common feature with a male victim is the extraction of sperm samples. The witnesses frequently dislike talking about this, but then give the distinct impression it formed the focal point of their whole examination.

Also worth noting is that these alien medical tests often involve two types of entity. It is commonplace for small creatures to do the actual examination whilst one or two larger, more human-like figures appear to supervise and engage in direct contact with the witnesses.

In British cases this same pattern recurs often. Alan Godfrey, the Todmorden police officer, reported it in his 1980 abduction. The family from Aveley in Essex in 1974 say that they were examined by small, ugly beings but the taller, blue-eyed entities were in obvious control of the situation. And so it goes on, case after case.

This pattern is not widely appreciated by the public, who more often think that alien contacts only involve one entity type (the small grey beings found in movies such as *Communion, Fire in the Sky* or *Intruders*). That the truth is more complex and yet still widely recorded may be significant proof of the reality of these experiences.

Peter, an American abductee, described his medical examination to the MIT symposium. He reported how two small creatures probed him on a table or bed, but that a taller entity was standing off to the side watching all of this and monitoring what the other beings were doing.

The small creatures pushed Peter's testicles to one side then inserted a tube into him. There was no evident pain, but when it was extracted and fluid was drained from his body he was left feeling humiliated. A cup-like device was also placed over his penis and semen was sucked into this repeatedly. As if to soothe his embarrassment the entities told Peter that this – at age nineteen – was the only time they would ever have to carry out such a procedure. They would contact him often in the future, but 'it will be easier after this'.

He was also told that these entities are intrigued by our higher emotions and spiritual feelings as these make us different from any other species. That is why the aliens often appear to challenge us emotionally during the encounters. It is all part of the experimental testing.

These isolated cases seem to form a part of a long-term pattern that began in October 1957, when a Brazilian farm-hand, Antonio Villas Boas, was spacenapped by small entities. He reports being seduced by a red-haired being who barked and yelped like a dog. Then he was left in a strange environment with cold temperatures and gaseous vapours. This suggested that he was being used in some sort of medical experiment. The female entity subsequently advised Boas by way of a gesture that she would have his child when she was back in the sky!

Boas was subjected to considerable medical appraisal, where symptoms akin to mild radiation sickness were discovered. Afterwards he developed his intellectual skills and qualified to be a lawyer. He also claimed several years later to have been invited to the USA by government sources to be shown a crashed UFO or alien bodies; although he refused to discuss what he saw even with members of his family up until his death in 1992.

The Boas case was not made public by its investigators for seven years. They realized that it was unique and wanted to see if it was followed by another like it. Two cases would offer strong evidence of some alien reality. One isolated example could be dismissed as a male fantasy.

That second case was the famous experience of mixed-race American couple Betty and Barney Hill, both spacenapped from the White Mountains of New England in September 1961. They had only partial memory but recalled under hypnosis later how both were medically examined – Betty being given what she was told was a pregnancy test and Barney seemingly having body fluid samples taken. The small entities which this couple met seemed very interested in the different racial background of the witnesses.

Then, in 1965, a male gynaecologist in Venezuela was visited by the tall blond entities, who displayed their abilities to perform what we would call magical or psychical experiences (e.g. materializing and dematerializing without the need for a UFO). They informed him of their desire to try to develop an inter-species breeding programme, if possible, and that their aim was basically friendly towards us. However, they interestingly warned of a second species of small entities who were engaged in a less positive relationship with humanity. The implication was that these, whilst not overtly hostile, would be less concerned by the implications of their activities on earth.

In December 1967 a police officer met aliens in Nebraska, USA, as they sucked power from overhead transmission lines. He was told about their magnetic propulsion system and also that they were operating a 'breeding analysis program'.

Within three days in October 1974 came two cases. A hunter was spacenapped in Rawlins, Wyoming, and was sent back by the entities – he felt partly because of the vasectomy operation that he had undergone. Then a whole family in Essex, England, were abducted, shown the magnetic propulsion system of the UFO and told 'we reproduce through you. You are our children'.

On 15 October 1979 an older woman and the young male friend of her son were on a quiet road in Brazil when they were spacenapped. She had hair samples taken, was given a gynaecological examination and then told that she was no use to them. But the 25-year-old man was then seen with tubes inserted and blood being taken from him. She was told that he was suitable for their purposes and would be kept. Then she lost consciousness and recalls nothing further until both were back in their car. The young man did not recall what had happened inside the UFO.

A 77-year-old man became one of the oldest known abductees when he was taken from a canal bank near Aldershot, Hampshire, on 12 August 1983. He was studied under a glowing instrument and then told to leave because he was 'too old and infirm for our purposes'. He died not long afterwards.

And so it goes on, right up to the 1990s – where, for instance, in 1992 an airline pilot met the small grey entities in his kitchen in Hungary and had blood and body fluid samples taken for alien purposes.

The impression one gains from all of this is of a gradual attempt to find a way to use human sperm in some alien breeding process. At first a direct sexual intercourse experiment was tried. This may not have worked too well, so in future cases only samples were taken. There appears to have been a series of probing sessions where the differences in human physiology were to the fore of study (there is evidence, for instance, that at this time aliens became interested in homosexuals and non-reproductive sex). As they experimented this way, the entities occasionally told witnesses about a 'breeding programme' in progress. Eventually, by the mid 1970s, anyone who was not young, healthy or capable of full and normal reproduction was apparently not considered suitable and so rejected. A steady programme of male spacenapping then followed, with the ages of between eighteen and twenty-five – i.e. the peak of male sexual maturity – being those that produced the most victims.

It is difficult to face this barrage of stories and not be shocked. Of course, various options could explain it, but one likely reason for such a pattern is unnerving. All over the world we find people who do not know one another and who are often reporting features that have only recently been made public knowledge. Yet all are saying much the same thing. Is that because – fantastic as it seems – alien experiments are really going on?

7 Alien Violations

When Ros was twenty-one she had a close encounter with a UFO. It literally changed her life. In the immediate aftermath she stopped menstruating and – according to medical opinion – she is now unable to have children. This terrible event seems to date back to the day in September 1982 when she became one more victim of the modern epidemic of spacenapping.

That day Ros was driving with her boyfriend from East Anglia to Northamptonshire. Near Sudbury in Suffolk strange lights appeared in the sky. The next thing she knew they had swooped down beside the car, whose engine and headlights were failing. A huge light that was very bright but did not hurt the eyes filled their view. Then it was gone and the car returned to normal. The couple drove on, but reached their destination to find three hours of time inexplicably unaccounted for.

Ros told her story – not to make money, nor to become famous and only after years of silence. She is now a very successful businesswoman and happily married. She has no need of either fame or fortune and, indeed, regards media attention about her UFO story as a serious distraction that could even lose her money through reduced customer confidence.

Having met her, I do not have doubts about her sincerity. She has undergone an awful experience and yet the tendency of most human beings when faced with a story like it is to smile, assume the witness is somehow deluded or just making it all up for some reason or another. Whilst, indeed, there are witnesses for whom such descriptions might apply, Ros is clearly not one of them.

In fact, in my experience, very few of these people are anything other than completely sincere and badly misjudged by the majority of their peers. We owe it to them to take their experiences much more seriously than we presently do – if only on the most basic premise that, from all we know, these things can happen to anyone and the next victim might well be you!

After her nightmare journey Ros only had sporadic dreams to suggest the true strangeness of what had happened during the missing time. She drew the inside of weird rooms, some kind of propulsion system and compiled worried notes about ecological disasters that could be waiting for the world.

Her response to this was sadly typical of the spacenap victim, especially those who are young women. She bottled it all up inside, could talk to nobody about her fears and effectively locked herself away from the world. All she had for company were her incomplete memories and sketches of the small, grey/blue-skinned entities with huge black eyes that had appeared like flashbacks in her mind.

Ros was lucky. Although she bore both the mental and physical scars, she met a man who understood her and they settled down together. Through hypnosis she did later explore some of the missing time and a memory emerged that plugged a few gaps. It is unclear if this helped or made matters more discomforting. However, under hypnosis she not only visualized the medical experiments by the little creatures, but – true to the pattern that is now repeating itself like a cracked record (but which Ros had no knowledge of when she explored her nightmare past) – this victim once again saw a tall, more human-like figure. That second being examined her gynaecologically. He inserted a long needle into her stomach and extracted samples, which appears to be the source of her subsequent medical problems.

Now Ros just hopes that by sharing her story she might somehow help others who have gone through a similar procedure. Whilst her case is one of the most extreme in outcome, it is by no means atypical. Yet her courage and perseverance show that you can go through it and come out the other side – irrespective of what explanation you seek to put upon these cases. In Ros's case she became a virtual recluse after her experience.

Maria Ward, from Kent, was rushed to hospital and treated as a victim of rape – the only time (to my knowledge) that this has happened in Britain; although there are almost certainly other examples of women who feel sexually violated but who may not have admitted (even to themselves) that the perpetrator of that crime was not a human being.

Maria alleges that in November 1990 a dazzling beam appeared in her bedroom, a voice told her to 'follow the light' and she began to float upwards and could see the ground down below. She regained awareness inside a strange room where she was in the company of small hairless entities with large dark eyes and another, more human and taller being who used powerful ESP to read her memories and emotions. Meanwhile the smaller beings conducted medical experiments, notably placing a probe into her navel and a worm-like instrument that moved about inside her womb.

When she recovered consciousness, Maria was back in bed and covered in blood and wounds. She was rushed to hospital and treated as a victim of a sexual assault. She chose not to enlighten the doctors as to what had really occurred but the hospital notes do include odd comments that: 'I can find no logical cause for these injuries ...' and 'I have never seen these types of injuries prior to this time.'

In the USA several studies by psychologists have established that women who undergo a spacenapping experience react almost exactly like victims of rape during the aftermath. They suffer identical problems coming to terms with the violation, by not talking to others, or having difficulty re-integrating into society and so forth. But there is a far more serious problem that confronts alien abductees. Most people understand, and are highly sympathetic towards, a woman who has been raped. Yet if that same woman were to allege that her sexual assault came by way of aliens, then she would be neither understood nor sympathized with by much of humanity. As such these spacenapping victims are forced even further underground.

The consistency of stories such as those told by Ros and
Maria and the way in which they also fit the relevant
stories from spacenapped males is extremely chilling.
Again and again the same features crop up. It takes a lot of
suspension of inherent disbelief to accept that these cases
could even possibly be real – that they are not just some
exotic fantasy. But it takes even more effort to dismiss out
of hand all these patterns that weave the tales together.
Realistically speaking they do seem to indicate that these
people may well, somehow, be relating some kind of
awesome truth.

We can see this pattern repeated all over the world.

Two women – Debra, a graphic artist, and her mother,
Pat – were working in Debra's home in Johannesburg,
South Africa, into the early hours of 19 July 1988. They
were endeavouring to finish an advertisement they were
contracted to design. But at 3.30 a.m. Pat decided to call it
a night and Debra drove her home. About seven minutes
later, as they approached Pat's house, a light appeared
behind them then zoomed straight at and engulfed the
car. Debra recalls throwing her head into her arms and
onto the steering wheel in a reflex response to what
seemed an imminent collision.

After this memories became confused, but they do recall
a mist, finding themselves inside a room and an
examination table set out in the midst of this space. The
entities they saw were small with no hair on their heads.
Some were male and others female – a female one, calling
herself Meleelah, was supposedly in charge.

The obligatory medical examination was carried out on
both women – including a scan over their bodies by a
bar-like instrument and a long needle inserted into the
area just above the abdomen, from where they were told
DNA samples were being extracted. The great pain that
this caused was eased by one of the entities touching the
women's forehead and causing it to magically disappear.
This kind of faith healing is not uncommon in these cases.

Keith Basterfield reports an excellent case from South
Australia, which involves a nurse. She had several close

encounters and was first abducted from her Port Augusta home in 1969 when aged about ten.

The woman (Susan) had a fragmented memory of this the next morning and more details surfaced through nightmares as she grew older. Eventually she underwent a mild hypnosis or relaxation therapy technique to try to retrieve as much recall as possible.

Susan had swopped beds with her sister that night and the entities reacted with bemusement at this event, as if they knew which bed she should be in. But she describes how a high-pitched noise was accompanied by the arrival of several small creatures and one taller, more human-like being, who communicated with her by telepathy and urged her not to be afraid. You will note just how often this small entity/large entity partnership is being reported with almost always the larger alien being the one using ESP and psychic powers to calm women down.

To get to the UFO, Susan was swallowed by a ball of light and then floated out of her bed and through the walls of the house as if they did not exist. A table was present in the UFO and she was medically probed by the taller being, who focused particularly on her vagina. After this Susan became unconscious and awoke, an unknown time later, feeling ill and being given a purple drink by the smaller entities (who, as so often is the case, seemed to act like menials under the supervision of the taller being).

After the medical, in another scenario that is reproduced time after time in these cases, Susan was shown images on a screen. These depicted a strange world and some form of terrible disaster. The entities seemed intrigued by her reactions to this 'in-flight' movie. Then Susan was told that she had to go back, but that she would grow up with an important job to do. She knows that she has met these entities many more times in her life.

Her descriptions of the two kinds of being are once more all too familiar. The small ones were around four feet tall with no hair and large eyes coloured dark blue or black. The taller one was up to seven feet in height and, aside from evident psychic powers making him almost like a magician, he was relatively human-like in form. He could pass in the street for human – which, if many of the contactees we have met earlier in this book are to be believed, is exactly what sometimes does happen.

Susan recalls that after the age of fourteen her spacenappings became more overtly sexual in nature. The entities extracted fluids and began to examine and then 'mess about' with her ovaries.

Keith Basterfield is commendably objective in his study of this case. He points out two things which could be of considerable importance to any understanding of what took place.

Firstly, Susan has the typical profile of a spacenap victim. She is of above average intelligence, has a phenomenal early life recall, is visually creative, with an active imagination and an eidetic memory (i.e. she can picture scenes in her mind and retain these in great detail for long spells). She also has a lifelong track record of paranormal experiences involving phenomena other than her UFO activity.

But, in addition, Susan was sexually abused in human terms whilst she was a child – a pattern that has been noted by researchers in a few other cases.

Some researchers suspect that a recall of 'normal' sexual abuse is a cover story invented by the mind to replace the more horrific one of abuse by aliens. An alternative is that the alien abuse memory is an attempt to distance the victim's recall from its true source – which might, on occasion, be a close family member.

Either way this is a key point to take into account; although it must be stressed that only a small percentage of abductees (unknown as yet but believed to be no more than one in ten) also have a history of sexual abuse.

Nevertheless, if this remarkable evidence does all favour a psychological explanation, Basterfield is willing to admit some points that might refute the argument. Susan's sister, for instance, recalls seeing a ball of light in the bedroom. Equally, after describing an abduction where the entities put something into her mouth, a routine dental X-ray depicted an anomalous shadow existing there.

I have seen that X-ray film. It does look very odd. However, a subsequent X-ray by different equipment failed to show the mark. Susan says the aliens came back for the 'implant' in between X-rays. The dentists are unsure whether the first plate merely formed a shadow on it during development.

Just as with male spacenap victims, we can look at the history of the female abduction phenomenon and trace another frighteningly consistent pattern behind these cases. This has emerged from reports which have often had little, if any, publicity – certainly not before very recent years, which is often long after they were first recorded.

Betty Hill was the first female victim that we know about. When she was taken from the White Mountains of New Hampshire, USA, in September 1961 she was told that the probing of her body with a long needle was a 'pregnancy test'. Later, techniques to extract eggs from a woman's body were perfected by human doctors and there were striking similarities to the medical examinations that female abductees were describing.

On 3 May 1968 a 19-year-old nurse's aide, Shane Kurz, was woken by her mother after seeing a UFO. She then lost consciousness, waking later in her Westmoreland, New York, home.

That a spacenapping might have occurred was evidenced by muddy footsteps leading to her room from outside. But it was several years of both physical and mental torture that led to the unlocking of deeper memories.

Not only did Shane have migraines and red rings around her abdomen, but she stopped menstruating for a year. She was under study by a gynaecologist in Uttica, who was baffled by her problem, but it righted itself gradually and within five years of her abduction Shane was back to normal – at least physically.

Hypnosis in January 1975 was conducted by Dr Hans Holzer. This fleshed out her nightmares and revealed an apparent memory of being taken into a strange room and forced to lie on a table by small white-skinned entities with large dark eyes and no hair. Throughout, the terrified young woman kept repeating that these beings claimed to know her. She remembers asking of the main examiner, 'But how does he know me?'

The entities used a long needle placed into her abdomen to extract samples of fluid. They told her that she had been chosen to give them a baby, or, as they elaborated: 'We are studying you ... We want to see if we can.'

Interestingly, she also had a memory of a 'rape' scene, but it is not clear whether this was her mind using a cover image to protect her from the more clinical procedure that only emerged under hypnosis.

Another female rape memory emerged from Mrs Verona*, a woman in her early thirties of Italian extraction but who was living in Somerset when the incident occurred on 16 October 1973.

Mrs Verona was driving over lonely moors near Langford Budville when her car engine stalled. A strange object was in some nearby fields and she was dragged towards this by a 'retrieval device'. She lost consciousness and recovered inside a strange room where some normal-height men with large eyes were using instruments like bars that moved across her body and employed needle-like probes to take samples of skin and nail. A huge suction device was place over her genitals and samples of fluid were sucked out.

After a while one of the figures returned and stuck a needle in her thigh (at which point Mrs Verona lost all power to resist). He then mechanically raped her and left.

This case was unique in British terms when investigated by Andy Collins and Barry King four years later. Mrs Verona had a near full recall, partly via dreams and nightmares. No hypnosis was ever used to elucidate her memory. She had arrived home that night with over three hours unaccounted for and it took great courage to tell her husband the truth. To this day she has never gone public with her story.

However, in early 1994 Barry King advised me of several subsequent meetings that he had with Mrs Verona where she reported a series of later visitations by the figures. Her teenage daughter had seen them too. Her husband had a period of missing time when he went behind a bush to urinate on a drive through Gloucestershire. Most interesting of all, she had had frequent nightmares about small, ugly creatures whom she now believed were the real source of her experience. She had come to believe that these memories, being so painful and horrible, had been buried deeper into her mind.

Does this suggest another possibility – that memories of extraterrestrial rape, such as those described by Antonio Villas Boas in Brazil in 1957, Shane Kurz in New York State in 1968 or Mrs Verona in Somerset in 1973 are only attempts by the mind to rationalize the incredible? Do they try to put a gloss of normality on top of the truly gruesome nature of the real alien medical procedures?

New York researcher Budd Hopkins has found in his work that some witnesses invent a mental 'cover story' to hide the truth. Often what first emerges is a missing period of time and some vague dreams, with an anomalous but pleasant image superimposed. These have included fields of rabbits surrounding a car, where the friendly rabbits replaced the real memory of small aliens that encircled the witness. In Whitley Strieber's case he recalls an image of an owl, where its eyes may have been the large alien eyes subsumed beneath this more acceptable memory. In one British case a dolphin in a swimming pool was the first memory encountered which seems to have played the same role of pleasant substitute imagery for a woman who was apparently abducted from her car on the East Lancashire Road.

Perhaps the alien seduction and the violence-free rapes reported in a few of these cases are just another level of defence set up by the mind – a second shell that aims to protect the witness from the rather more disturbing, clinical reality that lurks beneath the surface.

In January 1976 three women in a car in Stanford, Kentucky, claimed to have been abducted together. Two of them were in their forties and recalled only scattered images, e.g. of being studied by tall creatures or held in stasis. The third woman, Mona Stafford, who was ten years younger, reported finding herself on a bed and being probed by the creatures who, amongst other things, inserted a tube into her abdominal area. She felt her insides blowing up like a balloon. This is a not uncommon description of what the ova sampling operation seems to feel like.

The three women in this case were devout Christians and insisted upon taking a lie detector test when they reported the matter to the police. They passed this easily.

In November 1978 Elsie Oakensen, then also in her forties, lost fifteen minutes when her car was surrounded and stalled at Church Stowe, Northamptonshire. She recalls scattered images of being scanned and then rejected by the aliens.

Indeed, in every case where such a demeaning recall of alien rejection is involved it seems to involve witnesses like Elsie, or Luli Oswald in Brazil, or Alfred Burtoo in Aldershot, who are much older than the normal young profile of victims of these alien genetic experiments. Or else, as in the case of Carl Higdon of Wyoming, they have something else about them (in his case a vasectomy) which appeared to be a deterrent to the captors. This pattern is so strong and involves interweaving so many cases from all over the world that it is difficult to imagine it could emerge just by chance.

Even more remarkably, an hour or so after Elsie describes being 'rejected', and completely unaware of what had happened to her, four young women in a car at nearby Preston Capes also had a close encounter with a very similar-looking UFO that came down from the sky and affected their engine. These women have since been reluctant to explore the memory any further – if, indeed, there is any further memory to be explored.

As if to reinforce the targeting of young women travelling in cars, a third case occurred near Telford, Shropshire, in July 1981. The three women here were regressed separately and a near duplicate of the Stanford, Kentucky, case duly emerged.

One of the three recalled simply being held under observation. A second told of being studied for what appears to have been her emotional responses to odd events. Her captors were the typical more human-like figures. The third woman was given a full-scale medical examination by the all too familiar small, hairless, ugly creatures with large dark eyes. She spoke of the devices used that were scanning her body and the pulling sensation in her bones that other witnesses have also referred to. Although she did not have a full recall, she did add that the pain was focused in her lower regions and felt that 'they are taking something from my body'.

And so it goes on. A woman in Finland in 1980 was physically examined, told that she should support the peace movement and advised that these alien examinations – carried out by the usual small entities – were because they could not 'beget children' and needed human help.

Debbie Tomey, the young woman whose real-life abductions between 1977 and 1985 in Indiana were studied by Budd Hopkins and so inspired the (heavily fictionalized) 1992 TV mini-series *Intruders*, is another example. She told her story in almost identical fashion, reporting the gynaecological probes, the bloated sensation, the squeezing and pulling of her legs and the same small hairless creatures with the large, dark eyes.

In 1992 a nurse from Hungary was abducted from her house by strange little creatures and found herself on a table or bed under medical examination with samples being taken from her body.

Indeed, these stories are so consistent you can virtually write your own script by now. Is it really tenable that the wealth of human imagination would produce such an incredibly repetitive pattern?

However, there is an additional problem that we need to consider. These experiences – however they may be initiated – are filtered through the human mind. This is not a computer or video camera. It is an actively distorting, busily working organ. Witnesses have an unfortunate (if understandable) tendency to try to comprehend what has happened to them. They often read books or watch TV programmes about UFOs afterwards. Until recently there was little information available to contaminate their evidence. But today no case is uncomplicated by lack of awareness of what spacenappings are like.

An illustration of the problems this can create comes from a case that was first reported to me by Raymond Broderick of Clayton-le-Moors, Lancashire, then a reader of the magazine that I edit called *Northern UFO News*.

Ray told me how early that morning, 13 February 1988, a woman whom he knew only distantly as a neighbour had reported a terrible experience to him. She did so because of his interest in UFOs. This woman, whom we will call Bea, had been spacenapped at 2.30 a.m. by strange entities in silver suits. They had led her up a ramp into a UFO, where she was then placed on a table and examined by these beings who had leathery skins and smelt of cinnamon. Bea then awoke with a terrible soreness around her genitals.

Now I had a big problem with this case. The woman was clearly in great distress when telling this story. But I had seen – as Ray had not – a TV programme that was vital. It was aired just six hours before Bea claimed to have had her alien abduction and was an episode of the American soap opera *Dynasty*, in which the character of Fallon Colby relived her vivid spacenapping by aliens.

Fallon's story was clearly scripted with more than a little reference to Whitley Strieber's real case, published the year before. The aliens smelling of cinnamon is one example of that overlap, as this is a feature not reported anywhere, to my knowledge, before Strieber, but which *Dynasty* incorporated into the plot and which was now turning up again in Bea's case.

Of course, conceivably, this was a new aspect of these cases, or one that had been missed in earlier accounts. But there were other problems. The most worrying was how Bea told of being led up a ramp into the spaceship. This is just what happened in *Dynasty*, and is a staple of many science fiction movies where aliens kidnap human beings. It is, after all, a very dramatic part of the story and no self-respecting dramatist is going to miss showing that bit in gory detail.

The trouble is that real cases of spacenapping never (virtually without exception) actually include this aspect. It is so notable that folklorist Dr Eddie Bullard, who has studied 800 cases, has coined the phrase 'Doorway Amnesia' to describe the puzzling lack of recall about how witnesses get from their normal environment to the inside of a UFO.

My view here was that Bea had seen the soap opera,

perhaps had a vivid dream based upon it and had convinced herself that it was reality. As such I had great difficulty persuading any investigators to go and see her.

However, eventually Andy Roberts, Philip Mantle and Rodney Howarth did visit Bea. They concluded much as I had done; although they noted that the woman had a track record of strange experiences through her life and felt sure that she did consciously believe that her spacenapping was real. She had, it seems, watched the episode of *Dynasty* the night before.

The detailed report of what Bea claimed added fuel to the 'dream' theory. For instance, she offered the name of one of the entities as being 'Gerard' – hardly a typical extraterrestrial word. That was the clincher for me, because, although she had forgotten, I happened to know that Gerard was the name of the butler in the aforementioned TV programme!

And yet, other information poured forth from Bea's recall which was not a part of the *Dynasty* script. She told how the entities claimed they travelled for a duration of 150 light years (a light year is a distance, not a time period, but witnesses often report such astronomical absurdities).

As for the examination by the small entities, they 'shackled my legs up like, you know, when you're having a baby ... A long, thin thing with a light came over me ... Then the entity said, "She's been done." ' This apparently referred to the fact that Bea had been medically sterilized and the entity said to her after their procedure: 'Now you will be able to have a baby.'

After waking back in her bed, Bea felt ill and vomited profusely. She had three red marks like puncture wounds on her arm where she felt the tube was placed. Her genital area was also red and sore and covered in a white fluid, like shaving foam. This was confirmed by Ray Broderick's wife, some six hours after the alleged experience. Bea claimed never to have read a UFO book and these details are, of course, not part of a family TV show like *Dynasty*, nor, for obvious reasons, of Whitley Strieber's real experience.

So – this case was not as straightforward as it had at first seemed.

Ray Broderick later found that one of Bea's children

claimed to see the entities in the house and sketched them. He felt that what had happened was that Bea's abduction had occurred earlier in her life and had been buried deep in her subconscious mind. The viewing of the TV programme had triggered this into the open and produced a vivid dream in which she relived part of that memory but incorporated some spurious details from *Dynasty* – resulting in a confusing mishmash.

Frankly, at the time I could not accept this theory. It seemed like desperation. Today I am much less sure that it is impossible.

Bea was also later found by her GP to have a growth on her ovaries, which may, or may not, relate to this encounter. She also claimed a subsequent abduction in July 1988 when something was taken from her body.

This Lancashire case is just one more to add to the list, illustrating that what looks true on the surface may not be all there is to a story.

Together we have a frighteningly consistent set of data that seems to point in the same alarming direction. It is, of course, possible that these events are all hallucinations, vivid dreams or the result of watching too much TV. But can the patterns and the way these stories slot together so extraordinarily well all be blamed on nothing more than human imagination?

And, if it is only invention by the mind, why is it so confoundedly unoriginal and repetitive in nature? The human mind is capable of wonderful inventions – science fiction is littered with aliens of every conceivable shape, size and delineation. Yet these cases of spacenappings read like someone regurgitating the same story again and again. That has to be a real problem for anyone defending a psychological explanation.

For now, let us suspend all such speculation and assume that these cases do reflect some kind of basic reality. If there is an alien programme involving bodily tissue and fluid samples taken from victims during spacenapping, then what is the end result?

You will not be surprised to learn that the cases offer a startling conclusion about that too.

8   The Universal Mother

Let us return to the story of Bea, the Lancashire housewife and young mother. Hypnosis followed five months after her 1988 abduction memory; although not, I understand, with the support of the original investigators.

I believe it was conducted by a woman hypnotist under the auspices of the UFO group Quest, who are from Yorkshire. This process then elaborated on some of the details and included reference to an implement that was put inside Bea – 'It's going up. They're taking something from me ...'

The entity (now described as tall and human-like) explains that her visitors are scientists and just want to conduct experiments. They told her: 'They want this from me to make like we are families. They've taken something from me to make a family ... They want to make us over there ...' The interpretation of all this, it seems, was that the aliens are trying to recreate human beings on their own world, using their own genetic material somehow mixed in with ours because their planet is barren.

It is fascinating that exactly this concept has cropped up in case after case. Remember the woman in Finland in 1980 being told that the aliens cannot 'beget children', the wife of the family at Aveley in Essex told in 1974 that 'you are our children' (as part of a long-term experiment) or the gynaecologist approached in Venezuela in 1965 and informed that their medical experiments were designed to see whether it was possible to use human DNA to create some kind of alien baby.

Although it is often thought that this is a recent component of the spacenapping phenomenon, after it was first brought to light by New York researcher Budd Hopkins in his 1987 book *Intruders*, it clearly predates that by a long time. Indeed, from the very first spacenapping – of Villas Boas in Brazil in 1957 – the image of alien/human hybrid babies has stood out.

Hopkins' book reported on Debbie Tomey, the Indiana housewife, who had undergone a series of abductions from childhood onwards. This later took on astonishing proportions when she began to have a series of dreams which involved a strange-looking child. It had wispy hair and features that were a cross between human and alien (alien, in this sense, being the oval-headed, bald and pasty-faced creatures with large, dark eyes).

Debbie was drawn towards the terrifying conclusion that the child was real (not just a dream image) and the result of an alien experiment involving the use of her ova, human sperm and alien techniques (possibly including some added alien DNA), indeed that she was the child's mother; although used more like an incubator for the early period.

Hopkins checked and found that three other of his female spacenapping victims had undergone similar dreams, but had not mentioned them as they did not seem relevant. Without being prompted with details, they then offered up remarkably similar tales. Because the child was often of advanced intelligence and had a strange look to it, these vivid nightmares were given the name 'wise baby dreams' by Hopkins – and the hunt was on to try to place them within the overall reality of the phenomenon.

A typical case history would be the following example, from my files.

Corinne, a young woman from Birmingham, first had strange experiences at the age of eighteen months which, as you will not be surprised to hear, she recalls very vividly. She screamed down the household in the middle of the night to say that a small man was staring in at her through the bedroom window. They were then living on the third floor of the building. Ever since, Corinne has had a great fear of standing near windows at night, which suggests it masks a deeper memory that has not yet surfaced.

In childhood she had vivid dreams of a white face with

coal-black eyes and a tiny mouth. She knew this being, but could not recall how.

As she grew older her psychic experiences proceeded apace. These included frequent out-of-body episodes and a couple of occasions where she went into such a deep sleep state that her parents thought she was dead.

Other family members have seen things too. Her father reported a bright light pouring in through the bedroom window in 1987. When it vanished and he got up the courage to check, all the nearby street-lights were off.

Corinne had another experience where several small ugly creatures floated through her closed window in the middle of the night. They were 'grey and naked and extremely thin ... with expressionless eyes'. She picked up a can of hair lacquer from the bedside table and squirted it at them. This did the trick and frightened them off!

She first had wise baby dreams when she was in her late teens. These persisted for several years. In the dreams, as she told me in 1988, she gives birth to a strange and super-intelligent child. It has wrinkled skin, thin hair and ugly features. The entities whom she has often seen in her life tell her in these vivid nightmares that she is to look after this baby – which is a hybrid of alien and human stock – because they need to test her human emotional response to nurturing this creature.

Of course, Corinne regards this dream as being merely another case of Frankensteins in spacesuits – a fable told through her dreams. In the context of so many other cases like it, perhaps it is more than that.

In this case, Corinne could be accused of making up her story retrospectively. She approached me after reading my book *Abduction* and admits to having read *Intruders* as well. Whilst I do not believe she invented this or that she was aware of Hopkins' wise baby dreams when these experiences happened to her, that possibility can never be completely ruled out to the satisfaction of the sceptics. The mind can also, at times, adapt information to make it seem to fit in with later discoveries.

However, that same accusation is not possible with the case of Karen.

She had a whole series of psychic and UFO experiences,

including being rescued, 'guardian angel' style, earlier in life. In the summer of 1979 she had a close encounter with a strange ball of light whilst working at Pentire, near Newquay in Cornwall. A small time lapse was possibly involved. After returning to Cheshire she discovered that she was unexpectedly pregnant. On 16 September she had a dream of giving birth to a super-intelligent baby. This recurred several times and she became very concerned by the matter. On 26 December, Karen then awoke to find blood all over her bedsheets and doctors told her that she was no longer pregnant. It was assumed that she had miscarried in the night. Karen says, with considerable guilt, that she was relieved by this given the nightmares that she had endured.

Soon after the miscarriage, Karen met a strange man on the streets of Hyde. He smiled deeply at her as she walked past. She had a feeling of communication between them and that something was conveyed by what, on the surface, seems no more than a trivial encounter.

Then, in the summer of 1984, Karen heard a humming noise (exactly the same as had accompanied the blinding light she saw at Pentire). Outside the bedroom window of the Dukinfield home she then shared with her boyfriend was an egg-shaped object. A tall female entity with white skin, blonde hair and blue, slanted eyes lured her through the closed window and floated her into the UFO. The eyes of the entity seemed to hypnotize Karen as she felt compelled to follow. She knows that something important happened once she was inside the UFO, but cannot recall what this was.

Three years later, in early 1987, Karen woke in the night feeling a tiny hand of what seemed to be a child two or three years old holding onto her fingers. She felt good about this experience and urged her boyfriend to switch on the room light so they could see. He did so just in time to spot a tiny ball of light fade into wispy smoke and rise up through the ceiling.

This story was reported to me and I tape-recorded these details before Budd Hopkins first published *Intruders* later that year. At this time I had no knowledge of the wise baby dream syndrome that he was beginning to uncover in the USA and, therefore, I am virtually certain Karen cannot have had any either.

Female abductees becoming unexpectedly pregnant in the wake of a spacenapping experience is something that is surprisingly common. We have met it once or twice already. In one case, where I was sworn to secrecy by the young woman involved, she was adamant that this pregnancy had to be supernatural, because she did not even have a boyfriend at the time and had no sexual experience. She hid it from her family, but spontaneously aborted some weeks later. At least, that is, she was suddenly no longer pregnant.

Of course, in some of these cases we might assume that the woman was undergoing a false pregnancy, or, indeed, that if she was really pregnant this had a normal cause. She was just afraid to admit that to her parents – or even to herself. But this pattern occurs so frequently in close proximity to cases of spacenapping that we may well need to look beyond that simple explanation for the full answer to this problem.

Susan, from Port Augusta, South Australia, whom we met earlier, also had a phantom pregnancy in 1979 at the age of eighteen. Despite normal medical tests the condition could not be confirmed, although she briefly exhibited typical symptoms e.g. her periods stopped and her breasts became tender. She believes she spontaneously aborted with a show of blood several weeks into the officially non-existent pregnancy.

Seven years later, following an abduction experience involving sexual sampling aspects, she was positively confirmed as being pregnant. But she was adamant that this was impossible, as she had not had normal intercourse for many months. Immediately afterwards she began to have nightmares of giving birth to a strange-looking baby and was taken ill. Doctors later confirmed that she was still pregnant but there was no sign of foetal movement. A discharge of black material followed, which was diagnosed as a spontaneous abortion of the dead foetus.

In another Australian case investigated by Ray Brooke

and Keith Basterfield, a woman in her early thirties from Adelaide told how she had undergone a series of strange experiences in an odd room. In the last of these, in 1989, she was confronted by beings with thin bodies, grey skin and large hairless heads with slanted, deep and dark blue eyes. One of these beings was female and held a baby towards the woman. She was then asked by the alien to hold it and nurse the creature. This seems to have been the source of some interest for the watching aliens.

Yet, despite cases such as these, Basterfield still questions whether the phenomenon is real. He has conducted research, reported to the *Bulletin of Anomalous Experience* in June 1993. This suggests that of the 4000 or so cases of spacenappings that appear to have been documented by UFOlogists to date, only 9% of female abductees claim that they underwent an unexpected pregnancy immediately after an abduction. That is about 5% or so of all cases overall – or perhaps 200 spacenappings world-wide, of which only a dozen or so appear to have been fully documented and put on record.

Basterfield wonders if we might not be reading too much into the situation by making the alien human hybrid baby syndrome such an important part of the phenomenon on the strength of what is relatively little evidence.

In my own study of British cases this phenomenon has occurred four times to my knowledge in about fifty cases that I have recorded. That is about the same percentage as Basterfield suggests, given the proportion of female spacenap victims in my database.

However, I should add that these are cases that have been brought to my attention. I have never gone out and sought this sort of report from a woman and many witnesses would, understandably, never offer it up freely. Two of the four who have told me their experiences did so in strict confidence and only months after they had first shared their abduction memories with me, I think there are good reasons to suspect that it might be rather more common than we presently realize, but that the true statistics suffer for a variety of reasons. Not the least of these is that there are far more male abduction researchers than women and female abductees may well feel reluctant to discuss such intimate and emotionally traumatic details with a man.

If we piece these stories together the pattern that emerges seems to be this.

Women are first abducted as young children and 'selected' for later study. They may be conditioned through experiences of the psychic toy variety, or by having other quite friendly psychic phenomena, as if preparing them gently for the more traumatic events to come.

After puberty they usually find themselves abducted and studied gynaecologically, until, at the height of sexual maturity, perhaps between eighteen and twenty-five, ova samples are taken from them.

What happens next is less easy to ascertain, but from what some victims claim to have been told by their alien captors these ova are mixed with human sperm and genetically engineered by alien scientists attempting to develop a hybrid baby. Alien DNA may also be added. The result is then implanted back into the woman, who finds herself unexpectedly pregnant.

This whole process may surface in a variety of ways, but the fears of giving birth to an alien child seem to often manifest themselves as wise baby dreams. Some weeks later (often this is at about three to four months) the woman finds herself no longer pregnant and a spontaneous abortion is diagnosed. In fact another spacenapping has now occurred, during which the foetus has been removed – perhaps with some resultant blood loss left on the bedsheets.

What happens to the baby next is less well known, although the suggestions from some witnesses are that it is grown to maturity by the aliens in their environment (wherever that is). There is some evidence of it being occasionally shown to the woman after birth – at any point up to three years afterwards, although usually sooner than that. When this occurs, the aliens seem very interested in the emotional response of the woman to coping with the holding and caring for this alien/human hybrid.

Of course, none of this is presented as absolute fact.

That would be both foolish and impossible to prove. There could be other, perhaps psychological explanations for what is happening here. But this is the basis of a very consistent story about the reputed alien experimentation that seems designed to develop some kind of super-child. There is no doubt that the theory of this is well supported by anecdotal testimony of several dozen woman – and not a few men – coming from all over the world.

However, anecdotal testimony is a long way short of proof. What cannot be denied is that there is an almost total absence of medical evidence that any of these cases have really occurred in such a way that they have involved something paranormal producing the allegedly spontaneous abortion.

Dr Richard Neal, a California physician, has sought evidence for five years and tracked down many leads through investigators. Given his background he stands a better chance than most UFOlogists of gaining access to a woman's confidential medical records. Yet, to date, he has not come upon a single case where there is clear medical evidence of something unusual. Either there is no proof that the woman was ever pregnant in the first place or else there was nothing that could not be medically explained about the way that the pregnancy was terminated. Yet he continues to search for that elusive proof of what is known as the 'missing foetus syndrome'.

California investigator Ann Druffel reported on a typical case of what seemed, at first, to be very promising physical evidence. However, as soon as the medical records were tracked down it was found that the doctors had an explanation for the spontaneous abortion and that this apparently had no relevance, one way or the other, as to whether or not the woman had ever been spacenapped.

Ectopic pregnancies, for example, can occur when the egg attaches itself to the side of the woman's fallopian tube, as opposed to inside the womb. These are rare, and can be dangerous, and when they do occur may not initially give any obvious sign of pregnancy or of the eventual termination when they abort. The foetus often fails to grow normally.

However, despite these doubts, evidence continues to

come in. Psychologist John Carpenter reports on a case of an American woman who has had a deep phobia about dolls since her childhood. She would not let her own daughter have one in the house and would take them and destroy them in violent ways, such as by placing them on railway lines and letting trains crush them to small pieces.

After Carpenter investigated the woman's fragmented memories of UFOs and alien contact she described having a baby taken from her womb and grown to maturity by the aliens. She had projected its face onto the slightly distorted image of the dolls and come to feel hatred and fear towards them as a result.

In a recent case from Hungary, a woman was diagnosed as pregnant after an abduction experience and was even shown the baby on the ultrasound monitor. The head was unusually large in appearance. The woman was told that she had to have an operation to remove the foetus. The doctor then refused to confirm in public that the first scan had shown anything at all, even though the woman says that privately he knows what he saw but is afraid for his professional reputation if he were to admit what had taken place.

However, a gynaecologist I consulted advised me that the head of the foetus often looks abnormally large to an unsuspecting mother. Also that in some rare conditions which require the kind of abortion that may have been necessary in this case the foetus does take on an enlarged appearance as a consequence of the illness involved.

So perhaps some of these stories are misunderstandings based upon natural phenomena associated with pregnancy.

However, if these examples of alien hybridization are to be believed we must now ask: what happens to these babies after they have grown to maturity?

9 The Missionaries

In September 1989 I was honoured to be awarded with the title 'UFOlogist of the Year' by a huge gathering of people in Phoenix, Arizona. The cool fans of the hotel air conditioning battled against the hundreds of milling delegates and the sweltering desert heat that poured relentlessly outside. Phoenix had just set a new record for the number of consecutive days when the temperature climbed above one hundred degrees.

I was also fighting my own battle that day. For around me were seas of people whom I was desperately trying not to·dismiss as nutters. I was in the midst of the new age community which hosts these annual jamborees. Indeed, at nearby Sedona (a red rock gorge rising from the sandy terrain) they have built a whole town around their esoteric views at a spot which they believe matches an invisible 'spirit city' in some magical dimension. This had to be crazy. Yet these were nice people, who were evidently sincere.

As I lectured bravely about objective investigation, taking one step at a time, not jumping to conclusions that aliens had to be behind these UFO encounters, I was feeling not a little out of my depth. When asked about crop circles, then dotting English cereal fields with alarming regularity and the talk of the world, I uttered words that seemed like sceptical dismissals – referring to weather phenomena and (woe upon woe) that some of them were even hoaxes. I got pitiful looks back and was asked about the spiritual significance of the various shapes and patterns. Why were they manifesting themselves here and now? What was the message they were trying to convey?

So far as I was concerned this was much what I expected. I briefly surveyed the stalls set out with crystal power amulets and channelled messages from assorted alien worlds. These were neatly packaged onto cassette tape (just a few dollars a throw). I debated whether to spend $50 to attend a session with a mystic which promised revelations about which planet was my home, but chose the much safer option of indulging my passion for American Football and watching the Redskins play the Eagles instead.

This was how I had treated this sort of thing for years. However, what could not be denied was that there was an incredible lure attached to this attractive belief system. When UFOlogists who would call themselves 'serious' hosted a conference (where hard evidence and theories would be monotonously repeated) they could bring in up to a couple of hundred people. But take the new age approach and you would need a far bigger room. For every UFO group with half a dozen members there were half a dozen new age cults that were well into four or five figures.

It had never really occurred to me to question why. Perhaps I just assumed these folk preferred the easy option. I recognized people's need for an intergalactic cavalry to ride to the rescue and save the earth. If you were concerned by ecological disasters or political upheavals then our history offers precious little hope that we can sort the mess out for ourselves. To have a belief in friendly aliens who assure you that they will not let the inevitable happen and will arrive to save the planet at the eleventh hour seems a harmless and effective cure for paranoia.

Unless, of course, you bear in mind that there may not be any friendly aliens out there. It could all be a delusion – and, when the moment of truth arrives and the spaceships do not land, the earth might well just fall apart because of our own failure to act.

It should never be forgotten that when you turn over all hope to mythical superheroes who promise that they will save the day, then you get no second chance if Superman doesn't show up.

And yet, simmering at the back of my mind was the

feeling that there could be more to it than this simplistic view. Sometimes a thing becomes so universally popular because it hits upon a truth that everyone knows deep inside – like the global belief in survival of death. Maybe these new age beliefs about alien missionaries were striking a chord deep within the human soul and the time was exactly right for that revelation to be made.

It was a possibility – and one that at least deserved a hearing, I eventually forced myself to conclude. In a way this was what finally drove me to writing this book. For once I started to examine what these people were saying, once I analysed the coming together of various diverse ideas, once I really sat down and thought about it – then maybe, I had to admit, it wasn't quite so stupid after all.

Donna Butts is typical of what we are dealing with. I kept hearing about her case in mailshots from Dr Scott Corder, a Kansas GP. So convinced was he of Donna's story that he stuck his neck out and met with trouble from the state medical authorities. Yet still he stood by his guns. And I had ignored him. Maybe I owed him more than that.

Donna's adventures began before she was even born. In 1950 on their farm at Anthony, Kansas, Donna's mother and father were awoken in the early hours by a bright light. A huge triangle hovered over a barn and a glowing entity materialized in front of them. He offered a prophecy that the woman would have two children and the second would be a girl. That girl was being sent by the aliens as a missionary to spread some kind of word around the planet. As proof, a necklace with some alien writing on it was left behind. Donna's father never recovered from the shock and died not long afterwards.

When Donna was born, she was not told of her prophesied destiny until she was old enough to understand. Then, in November 1980, when she was married with children of her own, she had a terrifying close encounter. With her was her mother-in-law and two young boys. They were on a country road between Salina and Kansas City heading for hospital where Donna's husband was due to undergo surgery later that day. It was after 2 a.m.

Suddenly a light appeared in the sky and both they and

a truck in front responded to this by hitting the brakes and then trying to accelerate away from the craft. A beam of light shot out of the UFO and illuminated the road. The next thing they knew the truck had vanished as if it had never been there. Then – as if in the blink of an eye – they were driving into Topeka (a town we met earlier in this book, if you recall) and an hour of time was unaccounted for. Only this time it was an hour that had been added. They could not have driven from Salina to Topeka as quickly as they did.

Much later under hypnosis Donna discovered that she and the car were spacenapped and, whilst she discussed her mission with the aliens, her mother and the children were left to sleep in the car. The aliens then returned the car to the road outside Topeka – hence the faster than expected journey.

Four years later Donna met a tall man with blond hair whilst at the laundromat. He said he was called Peter and over subsequent meetings offered much knowledge about space and of the aliens' mission of peace. He claimed that the earth was going through the 'end times' up until 1995. She was an important mouthpiece for their rescue plans.

Peter has also been seen inside the house, surrounded by sparkling lights, and her children called him 'the starman'. He has often led Donna to the UFOs where she has met her alien guide called Neeki. On these visits she has been shown much about the future but also voluntarily agreed to have an implant placed inside her.

As you can see this case is very much like a cross between the contactees of the 1950s, who created many of the cults that still exist today after frequent chats with alien friends, but also with modern tales of spacenappings. These add the details of forced abduction and implantation – indeed, the truck was apparently found in the middle of a field by investigating police some time after the 1980 abduction; although there was no sign of its driver.

Of course, the image of a child being groomed to do a job for the aliens even before its birth is in keeping with the concept of the genetic engineering programme that has post-dated this by several years.

I have to admit that the Donna Butts case has many similarities with a story I had taken more seriously – if for no other reasons than I have spent some time looking into it and it happened in Britain. But if I treat that case as anything more than a tall tale, then there is no reason to be as dismissive of Donna's trip from Kansas into a land somewhere over the rainbow.

The British case dates from November 1957 – in fact only days after the Villas Boas spacenapping seduction had occurred in Brazil, but when few (even in South America) could possibly have known about it.

Cynthia was married to a sheet-metal worker and lived in the suburbs of Aston, Birmingham. She was twenty-seven with two young children, and claims that she was visited on a number of occasions over the space of fourteen months by a tall man with long blond hair who just materialized in her living-room. He scorched a newspaper with a kind of electric discharge as he first appeared. Just before this arrival a one-hour time lapse occurred – explained later as a 'failed attempt to communicate'. The entity was also seen by Cynthia's daughter (aged four) and claimed he was from Gharnasvarn.

The alien offered masses of information to Cynthia during his appearances – ranging from philosophies about space and time, preaching of peace messages and scientific knowledge (e.g. an alleged cure for cancer involving vibrating atoms). This went way above her head. It came through telepathy and Cynthia was also told that she had been selected because she had a mind that these entities could 'tune into'.

The being showed images to the woman on a three-dimensional TV screen that opened up in thin air and appeared exactly like a hologram – even though we had no such invention in 1957.

Poor Cynthia was pretty embarrassed by all of this. The last thing she wanted was to become a cult leader or missionary, and kept telling her visitor exactly this.

Interestingly, on all bar his first two visits, the alien did not arrive in magical fashion – but via the front door! He was wearing earthly clothing and could have passed in the street for a normal, if rather handsome, tall blond-haired, blue-eyed man. Cynthia called him a 'Greek Athlete' – which is a good description of these 'aliens who are living on earth' that we keep hearing about from witnesses throughout this book – although this is one of the earliest known examples.

Towards the end of these visitations the alien made a startling pronouncement. In September 1958 he told Cynthia that she was pregnant and that, although her husband was the father, the child was 'of the race of Gharnasvarn'. Exactly how this was to come about was never elaborated on. Cynthia was dismissive, not expecting to be pregnant, but a subsequent doctor's visit confirmed that she was. Her visitor gave the body weight, delivery date and sex of the child – only days after what must have been conception. She was told what to name him (for it would be a boy) and that he would grow to be a great influence on mankind.

The child was born the following summer, as predicted (although a couple of days late and one ounce different in body weight). Not surprisingly, she followed the alien's advice as to the name for the child and after that her visitor never returned.

All of this was indisputably put on record in 1958 and 1959 – before the child's birth; although it is an aspect of the case little known to modern UFOlogists. At the time it seemed difficult to interpret and made little real sense. Viewed forty years on it looks a whole lot different.

Of course, what this means is that somewhere out there is a man now presumably in his mid thirties who is the subject of another alien promise – just as Donna Butts in Kansas apparently was. I have purposely not given this man's Christian name here, as he may not wish to be associated with this story. I have tried to trace him, but so far have not succeeded. It will be very interesting if he can be found and he does have an opinion to offer.

Reluctant missionaries seem to be everywhere.

Lorne Goldfader of UFORIC, a research group in Canada, told me about a case that he uncovered in a peculiar way in Vancouver.

In October 1992 he gave some UFO material to an office clerk that he barely knew. This was on impulse and for no apparent reason, but she then contacted him a few days later to say that she felt that her story could be important.

In early 1993 the investigation of this affair proceeded to regression hypnosis where an account of lifelong abductions – beginning at the age of two – came forth in the usual way. During these visits to the UFO she was told that her genetic structure had been altered whilst she was just a foetus inside her mother's womb and that this process had adapted her to be a kind of mouthpiece for the aliens in the times to come. This purpose and mission would only be revealed when the time was right. Until then it would remain buried in her subconscious.

Peter Gregory of Lincolnshire sees things a little differently. He has always had psychic experiences and has indeed been called upon to use his powers to find missing children and so forth.

After moving to Mablethorpe he found himself surrounded by UFO experiences and succeeded in video-filming triangular lights twice during the summer of 1993. On 9 December the many sightings that were unfolding around him became so intense that the local media were inundated by reports of huge triangles floating around Louth and surrounding villages. House lights switched on and off and TV sets changed channels as the objects flew overhead. Even the station commander at RAF Donna Nook saw this and Nick Pope of the MoD confirmed to me, on 10 January 1994, that 'there was no obvious explanation for these sightings, and no military activity that might tie in. As far as I am concerned, these sightings remain unexplained'.

During his encounters psychic events began to occur around the Gregory household. These included a baby's pram rotating on its axis all by itself and a glass exploding into fragments on a shelf with such force that pieces were thrown eight feet into the air and fused together as if by great heat.

He also alleges that he has been contacted by the entities behind the encounters and has learnt much about their purpose. These entities, which he first saw on 16 April 1993, were human-like – about six feet tall, very thin and with long, blond and reddish/brown hair. The eyes were a piercing blue.

These entities showed him scenes of ecological catastrophe in the earth's future, where no life remains on the planet. This seemed to indicate that their task was to try to prevent this cycle from happening.

Peter has created a group called Skywatch, banding locals together to try to bring awareness of this phenomenon. Interestingly, he does not perceive these aliens as being from outer space but rather as more closely related with our earth – possibly from another dimension or our own future. He feels that they select certain people with psychic abilities, communicate with them and then try to use them as a medium to express their message.

However, it has to be said that Peter Gregory's brand of contacteeism is different from most. There are dozens of evangelical contactees who tour the conference circuits in the USA, record cassette tapes and try to change the world for the better with their 'preaching'. They are almost always in contact – so they believe – with people from the stars – Orion, the Pleiades cluster and alpha centauri being the most popular locations.

The names these entities offer are also often, frankly, daft – at least to a cynic's ears. We hear of Oxalc, Andromeda Rex, Rama, Aura Rhanes, and so forth. It is difficult to get over the impression that such entities would be more at home in a Dan Dare comic strip.

A few of these people have become famous, thanks partly to Oscar-winning actress, Shirley MacLaine, whose trips to Peru where she met some of these 'channellers', as they are also called, have been well documented in her delightful autobiographies. She certainly takes them seriously and has interacted with the new age UFO community on a strong level now for years.

Nevertheless, for every contactee who has gone public with their story and filled a niche within the new age lecture circuit in the USA, there are a dozen more who would never dream of such self-promotion. More often than not the name of the game cannot be said to be a search for fame and fortune. Instead it seems to be a quest for personal understanding and a quiet attempt to put across what has happened just to someone who might listen without bursting into laughter.

A woman from Walsall reports, for instance, how a stranger in the park told her that she was in contact with a group of small entities who called themselves 'genetics'. They use this term, because, as they told her, 'we were genetically created on our craft using human tissue'. They had a great task to perform on earth and this had involved the use of religious leaders throughout history – including Jesus.

Moreover this woman had a daughter whom, she claimed, had been exchanged for an alien! The girl was in her pram in the garden at the age of nine months when she screamed out loud. When the girl grew older it became clear that the child felt that she was somehow 'different' and that, in fact, she had relinquished her body and allowed an alien entity to take it over during that brief moment in her pram. The purpose, allegedly, was so that the alien being could live – through this girl – during the period of great crisis that the earth was about to face.

In isolation this story seems another absurd one on top of quite a few wild tales that you have read so far. Of course, it is not in isolation. Not only does it make a vague sort of sense, given everything else that we have looked at in the past few chapters, but it actually has much more of a parallel with the work of Ruth Montgomery. This is not well known in Britain and may well offer independent corroboration. What she has to say is just another piece of the jigsaw that helps to identify the picture that we are trying to put together.

Thirty years ago Ruth Montgomery was a famed Washington correspondent who mixed regularly with politicians and world leaders. She worked on a book about renowned psychic Jeanne Dixon, who had, for instance, foreseen Kennedy's assassination. That event was to have a profound effect on Ruth's life.

Afterwards Ruth began to receive automatic writing. An entity took over her body and wrote philosophical scripts through her. From these messages Ruth composed a series of best-selling books around the theme of survival of death and carved out a new career for herself.

However, from the late 1970s onward odd things started to flow out of her channelling from these guides. They reported what they called 'walk-ins' who, it seemed, were examples of friendly spirit possessions. Just as evil forces may take over someone's body, so, the claim went, good spirits could do the same – with the permission of the current tenant, of course!

In her book, *Strangers Among Us*, Ruth reported on what her guides had told her about this weird phenomenon. How there were people, many unaware of it, who were not the original holders of their bodies. They may have vacated them during a suicide attempt, or near death experience, when it was widely believed that they had survived. Instead their spirit had really departed and a wise old soul had leased their body. They wished to be present on earth in this time period without having to reincarnate first as a baby.

It was a bizarre idea, but one that is not quite as ridiculous as it seems when you bear in mind that most religions seem to accept the concept of possession by devils. Why not then be possessed by saints?

However, it was some time – the mid 1980s in fact – before Ruth Montgomery could accept the next step that was offered to her by the communications of her guides. She was told that some of the spiritual entities that 'walked-in' on a human body were not of this earth. They were aliens. Eventually she claimed to meet a number of people who were alien spirits locked in human bodies, having deliberately incarcerated themselves on earth during the coming few years of great tribulation.

This is the cornerstone of much modern contactee lore and of reports from spacenapping victims. They say that the earth is about to enter a terrible spell – of either natural or man-made disaster – and that during this phase millions of people may die, or suffer horribly. As a consequence, more and more alien walk-ins are taking control. She has even been told that one will ascend to the US presidency before the turn of the century!

This fits in disturbingly well with the image of the flood

of missionary contactees who have been implanted with some task to perform deep inside their subconscious mind whilst undergoing a near-forgotten alien contact. When the time comes these people will know what to do.

The great disaster is, by all accounts, due to be a shift in the poles of the earth. In an instant climates that are hot will become freezing and ice fields will melt into oceans. As a result coastal areas and island nations – such as Britain and Japan – will be devastated. Earthquakes will rip landmasses apart and volcanoes will be jerked into violent eruptions.

Supposedly this has happened several times in the past. Indeed, there is some sign within the geological record of rapid reversals in the earth's magnetic field which would accompany such a catastrophe. Some new age thinkers believe, for example, that the Biblical flood was a real event and have sought evidence of it from archaeological and geographical data all over the world. Others note the rapid demise of the dinosaur species 65 million years ago as another possible example of a sudden reversal of the poles.

If Ruth Montgomery's guides (and quite a few contactees and spacenapping victims) are all to be believed, this pole shift is inevitable and will occur within the next decade. All that the alien visitors can do is be here on earth in as great a profusion as possible to help humanity cope with the aftermath and ensure that the planet somehow survives.

It is a frightening thought, but then prophets have always foreseen doom at the turning of the millennium. Nostradamus, the astrologer, for example, speaks explicitly of the seventh month of 1999!

Specific given dates for these 'end times' have been offered by abductees before and have all passed without event. Many, for instance, referred to 1992 – which came and went without incident. Others now believe 1995 is going to be the date. Most just say it is very, very near.

Thankfully, Armageddon keeps getting postponed. But one day, of course, these prophets, spacenap victims, contactees and channellers just might be proven right. Then will the 'sequence of events' that one abductee referred to suddenly begin to unfold and will an army of hidden missionaries awake to their purpose in life?

10 Unlocking the Genie

Christine stood on the podium, staring at many faces blurred into one continuous crowd. There were hundreds of them, eagerly awaiting her next word. Unafraid, she was booming out into the auditorium, delirious and happy.

Somewhere in the background the cameras whirred, silently recording everything that happened in this lavish, splendid ballroom. Reporters from across the antipodes were scribbling into their notebooks and rehearsing crazy headlines whilst pretending to listen to what was said.

All of this was shifting out of focus. Christine could feel her state of consciousness moving from rock-hard, feet-on-the-ground mundanity to some higher plain that was like drifting up in the clouds above Mount Everest.

Interesting, she thought to herself. This is what it is like to enter an altered state of awareness. The thought seemed to pump her higher towards a new recognition where everything was possible. The words just tumbled out of her mouth and she heard them echo through the microphones and loud-speaker circuits as if they were coming from another room.

On a different day, in a different world, Christine would have called this person a crackpot – spouting as she was the claim that aliens were abducting humans. She would have defended resolutely the objectivity of her field; insisted with passion that you cannot reach ridiculous conclusions on the grounds of anecdotal testimony alone. To do so was to be weak. It meant that you had given in to the foe – wishful thinking. Didn't she know that people wanted aliens to be real? If you were writing or lecturing about this subject then the obvious thing to do was to give them what they wanted, if popularity was all you cared about. It was not to mutter on about proof and psychology or preach caution rather than acceptance.

Yet that was not happening here. Christine was freewheeling and the words were being transmitted directly from her inner self and by-passing her conscious mind. She was telling everyone a truth she did not even believe herself. The aliens *had* landed. They were here – now.

Let us stop this pretence. You know that Christine is me. I know it. I have been fumbling with this third person narrative throughout this book like a juggler with stage fright. You must have worked out – just as I have done – that I have adopted it, like the pseudonym which so many witnesses request, so as to avoid the open confrontation with the truth.

I have run from that truth for twenty years or more. The moment of revelation about this fear came as described above.

In a way it was ironic that it occurred where it did – or as it did – after years of writing about the 'Oz Factor' – an altered state of consciousness that marks a person's entry into UFO reality. For here I was – in September 1991 – sliding through my very own altered state just as I stood before a packed audience at the Sebel Town House, one of Sydney's finest hotels, resplendently situated in the heart of Australia. It was, very aptly, my own 'Oz' factor.

Early the next morning I jetted off to Brisbane, for a short layover. As the plane flew and I watched the clouds drift by my window I saw something extraordinary. It was not a UFO. In a way it was more important than that. I saw just what I had been fearful of for so many years. Why I had screamed so loudly that the existence of aliens was not proven – could probably never be proven. It was, at heart, because I knew how the evidence pointed so firmly in that direction and I was, frankly, scared to death of that awesome conclusion.

That evening, as the sun set over the Coral Sea, and I sat on my verandah in a new hotel in Cairns, I composed a letter to my friend Jerry Clark, then back in the USA. He was editor of the *International UFO Reporter,* having been groomed by the UFOlogist whom I had most admired and who had steered my career, the great scientist Dr J. Allen Hynek. I respected Jerry enormously and we had often debated the evidence. Whilst we agreed upon a lot of things, we had one profound area of dispute. He was convinced that some UFOs were alien craft and I, very definitely, was not.

Now I had to tell him what had happened to me. How I had just realized why I had been so sceptical. I had no idea if I would remain strong in my new-found philosophy. When I flew home and faced the chill winter of English UFOlogy, with its ice floes of deep reservation, I might crumble and revert into my shell. That's why I wrote to Jerry as I did. For I knew that there was no way back after that. I could never deny that one act later.

I also wrote a series of editorials in my magazine, *Northern UFO News,* during late 1991 and early 1992. It was fascinating to judge the reactions of my colleagues to these.

Predictably, one sceptical bastion took a line that other readers adopted less vociferously. They felt that it was the 'done thing' to profess personal experiences, citing a couple of other UFOlogists who were writing of their own adventures. The feeling seemed to be that this was because it paid better (both metaphorically and literally).

I understand that opinion. In their shoes I would have almost certainly felt the same way myself if I was reading the words of others. But, whilst I cannot analyse my inner motives, in so far as I can judge, this was not the reason behind what I have been saying. I am merely reporting things that have occurred to me and which may, or may not, be important, but which deserve more consideration than I have given to them before.

Other readers told me that they saw in my confessions a sign of schizophrenia. Again, I cannot judge that. I was certainly in two minds about whether to put these things down in writing, but I do not have any other reason to believe I am suffering in that way!

What was true, and what was pointed out to me, was that I had just undergone the most intensive pressure. The

12,000 mile flight to Australia is gruelling. Within minutes of my arrival I was doing my first radio interview and for days on end after that came a constant stream of TV chat shows, magazine photo calls and radio phone-ins. This was Australia's first international UFO conference and the media had gone to town. Then there were dinners and receptions organized by the Japanese financiers. By the time I opened the conference itself – by being unexpectedly forced to enter through a sliding door bedecked with flashing lights to the strains of the theme tune from *2001: A Space Oddysey* – I was virtually drunk on exhaustion. That no doubt had to be relevant.

Yet I am sure there was more to it than all of that. I am merely reporting events that are true to the best of my knowledge. Interpretation of these can only be left down to others. But I am as entitled as anyone to express my own view about them; which is that I think that I finally realized how I had tried to escape from a lifetime of oddities by raising a barricade of self-defensive scepticism. Perhaps I am wrong in this conclusion. But it seems to make sense.

So, let us review the patterns evinced in Christine's (that is *my*) story and add quite a bit more that was to come later. Then I will take you through the gradual process that I followed to try to unravel it all. In that sense I was doing what UFOlogists do every day when faced with a witness who proclaims some strange incidents buried within their past. Out of this emerges the evidence for the contacts, abductions, spacenappings and – to a large extent – much of the star child philosophy we are discussing in this book. So my account of how it slots together has a deeper significance than being just one more story to tell.

I entered into this research with an open mind and emerged with that more or less still intact. What I can do, therefore, is give you a first-hand perspective on the way in which half-forgotten memories are transformed into a half-believed-in experience. Then, with the advantage of twenty years' research combing through this kind of data, I can tell you what it felt like, describe how things fell into place and take a shot at trying to interpret what all of it means.

As you will see, my story takes on just the same

proportions as everybody else's in this book. It is strange. It is certainly hard to believe, just as much for me as it will be for you. Fortunately, I know that it is true. But I don't know the right way to interpret what it means.

Aside from the scattered childhood memories from Rossendale that I have presented in an earlier chapter, my first recall is of that night in Finsbury Park, London, when the big light came down.

After this I certainly developed an unusual interest in space, which rapidly transformed into the study of UFOs and aliens. I also wrote that strange story – *Sleep Can Take You Far Away* – at about that time.

There was also the UFO experience in Blackpool, in August 1963, which is so trivial – in that it has no conscious personal level to it – and yet has always been etched in my mind as of great relevance. I do not know why this is so. It may be that it masks something deeper inside. But that has always been just guesswork and may be no more than wishful thinking. However, I have checked records and there was a real sighting made in Blackpool that same night. So I did not imagine that an event had occurred. Something really happened that night and somehow or other it had a profound effect upon my life, if only by directing me into UFO research.

As I grew older I had various psychic experiences, which I have written about in my books. These included several precognitive dreams and one very frightening out-of-body experience when I was nineteen. At the time I was at university. This traumatic event upset me for weeks and indirectly precipitated my departure from the physics course that I was taking – leading me into teaching and from that into media communication work.

In fact, I should have been studying astrophysics at Edinburgh University when it happened. I passed the relevant exams and was accepted by the college. Days before I was due to leave Manchester I opted out of going north because I did not want to leave my boyfriend. At least that is the conscious reason my mind has always offered up. Instead I transferred to a less relevant course closer to home – with the result, one year later, that was described above. My friend left town soon enough anyhow. He married the daughter of a gold mine manager and emigrated.

I do not know whether I believe in fate or whether you are responsible for all the choices that are made in your life. I do suspect that had I gone to Edinburgh my life would have been very different. I cannot see me having become so ensnared by UFOs with that kind of career to contend with. Science and UFOs make uneasy companions.

Over the years I have seen quite a few UFOs – many with obvious solutions, such as aircraft lights seen through mist. I am often asked about them by the media and find it interesting that when I reply, it is always to talk about two of these experiences. Both of them were put on public record when they happened and I feel safe discussing them.

The only incident which I usually say has no clear explanation occurred in September 1980 when my boyfriend and I were on a motorcycle, riding from Hampshire to Cheshire. Passing south of Swindon we saw three lights form a triangle over what we later discovered was the Avebury stone circle. I always thought that these were parachute flares, but I let a sceptical UFO group investigate the matter and they failed to establish this fact. As such, they might have been UFOs, but as lights in the sky they were no big deal anyway. Interestingly, when I later asked him, Paul said that he had not experienced the sighting in the same vivid way that I had; although at the time I was convinced otherwise. He was, of course, driving the motorcycle and so could not pay quite as much attention as I.

The other event, in April 1978, is discussed in detail in my book *UFO Reality* as a good example of a glaring misidentification. I was living at Irlam, Lancashire, and waiting for Paul to arrive on his motorbike. As I watched from my doorstep, looking out across Chat Moss, I saw a yellow/orange ball of light, which hovered in the distance. At that time I had not become a writer and my UFO work was little known. So when a reporter arrived from the local paper he did not do so because I was a UFOlogist but because a woman walking her dog on the moss had seen the UFO and reported it to them. She had spotted me on the doorstep and offered me as a back-up witness.

When telling this story I always play down her account to the media – in which she described the light as a large craft with a transparent dome on top. I also report that I investigated and established that in truth it was a helicopter crop spraying over a mile away in Cadishead. There had never been more than an orange light present. Everything else that the woman claimed to see was down to her imagination. This was a prime example of how the brain decodes images via the senses and then evaluates them in an inappropriate way. It is an illustration of why UFOlogists love to say that 95% of all UFO sightings turn out to be mistaken identity – a fact I have certainly trotted out in almost every lecture that I have ever given.

Only, there is a problem. When I recently read back through my notes about this case I found something curious. Yes, I had checked at a local farm to find a helicopter crop spraying. Indeed, quite possibly, that is exactly what this UFO was. But – despite my insistence down through the years, and, indeed, the words that I had written into *UFO Reality* back in 1983 – I had never actually established that possibility as fact. In truth I was conning myself into believing that I had, presumably because that is just what I wanted to believe.

Whilst I still rebel vigorously against the very thought and feel sure that this probably was a simple IFO (Identified Flying Object) – perhaps even a helicopter – the fact of the matter is that I have no proof that what the woman told the *Warrington Guardian* that she had seen was not correct. Maybe she did have a close encounter with the craft that she described at very near range. Maybe I did too, but have blocked it out of my memory for some reason. This whole idea seems absurd, but – regardless of my bravado – I cannot demonstrate otherwise. I merely have spent sixteen years implicitly believing that I could.

What I never discuss with the media is another UFO sighting that I made – again in the company of Paul. This was in August 1977 and took place at Chester, where my boyfriend then lived.

This case is not secret. I can prove that I am not making it up retrospectively, because I wrote about it in the September 1977 issue of *Northern UFO News*, under the heading MY CONTACT WITH FLYING SAUCERS – WELL ALMOST! The words were, as you can see, deliberately belittling the tale.

I never went back to this editorial and avoided the memory of what happened in my mind. It was like a scene in a novel that just did not work and which you would rather skip past and get on to a good bit. However, here is the gist of what I wrote soon afterwards in that magazine editorial.

Paul and I were in a triangular wedge of field between the Chester to Crewe and Chester to Warrington railway lines. It was not far from his then home and we used to walk through it on our way back from spending time in this beautiful Roman city.

That night was warm and we were on the grass looking up at the sky talking 'when we became aware of a brilliant blue ball at the other end of the field. It was low and hovered seemingly just above rooftops. It then moved slowly to the side and hovered again. The blue was like that on a police car. Despite being within a quarter of a mile it remained just a ball'.

Paul and I were sure it was an aircraft, but became less sure as the sighting proceeded. Then, suddenly, the blue light vanished and two other lights (one white, one red and with a deep, slow pulse to them) appeared in its place. The object drifted away. Only then did we hear a faint sound like an engine and become relieved that it had to be an aircraft. Yet, as I pointed out, why had there been no sound when it was virtually on top of us?

Paul and I never talked about that night again, either with each other or with anybody else. There seems to be no reason for that. If it was just a misperception of an aircraft it ought to have formed another good anecdote for my lectures. Yet this one was clearly regarded as taboo for me.

Let us move on a decade, to 8–9 July 1987, when I knew far more about UFOs and had written half a dozen books on the subject. This was when perhaps the strangest experience of all took place. Because it makes no sense I have never talked about it openly. But it deserves to be put on record.

I had been lecturing in the USA and had, in fact, briefly met Whitley Strieber about two weeks earlier in Washington DC. After traversing the country I was now on the very long (three-day) train ride from Oakland, California, to New York City.

I had a tight connection in New York to make my flight back to Manchester, so was certainly worried when the Amtrak diesel broke down before we reached the platform end in Chicago. This threw us forty minutes behind schedule as hasty repairs were made. My mood was not helped by a young girl opposite me who was moving home from Sacramento to Syracuse and was taking her even younger sister with her for economy reasons. The day before, she reported, the train had reached New York seven hours late, 'because it had rained in Nebraska'.

I was very tired after two nights in my seat with little sleep. I recall passing through Cleveland at around 12.30 a.m. (allowing for the time zone change) and then – the next thing I knew – it was 6.50 a.m. and we were in Buffalo, New York. UFOs were certainly not on my mind. Indeed, I was rather foolishly trying to see nearby Niagara Falls in the morning dimness. However, it was just before reaching here that the dream occurred.

The dream was lucid, which means that it was more vivid than usual and my mind was fully alert throughout. I was aware of what I was dreaming, questioning all that I saw. I have had lucid dreams before – on rare occasions – but this was the only time that I have ever had one when not in bed.

In the dream I was on the train but there was a huge dome-shaped light beside the track. I thought it was a sports stadium and I was trying to figure out which NFL team this structure might belong to. However, there was something really odd about its nature. I had an urge to get out and walk towards the glow. I felt desperately keen to go inside. I was warm, happy, calm but also excited because within that dome was something I really wanted to experience – but I could not work out what that was.

Yet, in my mind, and I knew that this was not 'real', like the sports stadium was 'real', I could see lots of other people. I told myself – *no, you don't really want to leave this train. It's going where you want to go. Stay where you are.*

Then I realized that there were two figures by the side of the track, almost like highwaymen attempting to hold up the train. They were partly on and partly off the rails and the engine was gradually slowing to a halt. By European standards American trains travel quite slowly much of the time and so it did not take very long to become stationary.

The figures wore some kind of clothing that reflected light. It looked silvery, but I remember thinking in my dream that – unlike all the UFO accounts that I had read before – this wasn't as shiny as I had expected it to be. It was really rather dull. Equally, I knew these figures were alien and I also knew that they were interested in me.

That was it. I awoke in an instant with a start and jerked upwards in my seat, as if suddenly catapulted back into reality. There was nobody else around me. The girls were at an all-night party in the dining-car. Soon afterwards we pulled into Buffalo and my ill-fated desire to see Niagara shook me into full wakefulness. Only then did the memory of what had just occurred hit me hard in three different ways.

I knew it was a dream. I kept telling myself over and over that this was all it was. I remembered, without knowing any details, that Strieber had written of a train-board abduction in his book *Communion*. This was the only time that I had ever heard of such an unusual incident and the recollection came as a great relief, because it helped persuade myself that this must have been the catalyst for my own peculiar dream. Yet I was very keen to remember what else had happened after the two silvery figures stopped the train. Try as I might I could not get past that point in my dream recall.

The second thing I realized, and confirmed with my timetable, was that we were just over an hour late reaching Buffalo. We had been on time at the last town I had checked, having made up the time easily since Chicago. However, as you might imagine, an hour is neither here nor there to Amtrak's schedules when journey lengths are measured in terms of days. So, of course, there could be any number of explanations for the delay at this point and, as the guard told me when I asked him about it later, still worrying about my New York flight – 'I didn't even notice that we were late.'

However, certainly the oddest thing that struck me on awakening was a pain in my left thumb. I looked at it and saw a tiny cut about 12 mm from the tip. This was clean, not deep and was later measured as 3 mm long. It formed a reverse tick mark in shape and there was no blood at all. It was already healing and the pain, which was initially quite intense, faded rapidly and was completely gone within minutes.

I reacted in a quite bizarre fashion to this mark. I literally scoured the seat, the armrests, the windows, everywhere, until in the end I was near desperate with panic to find a cause. I simply had to trace what it was that I had cut myself upon. But, try as I might, I could find no sharp edges. I felt really depressed when unable to dispel the oddness of this cut.

I showed the mark some forty-eight hours later to my colleague Peter Hough upon my arrival back in England. I also told him the above story. The cut was plainly visible but a week later it was fading fast. Within a fortnight it was very difficult to spot without knowing exactly where to look.

I am well aware how trivial this sounds. I am not professing that there is anything supernatural behind these various accounts. But nor do I have any rational solutions beyond the obvious ones of dreams or coincidence.

However, my main point is that this sprinkling of strange phenomena is no more and no less than what most witnesses have to offer when they approach a UFOlogist. They come, wondering deeply whether behind such flimsy memories lurks something truly weird.

As such, these events – be they something or nothing in the final analysis – do provide the perfect starting point for a safari into the darker recesses of the human mind. I decided that the time was right to explore them further and see what might emerge. I would unlock the genie.

I should stress that this was not done because I wanted to be an abductee. From all I know about this phenomenon it is not something to be desired. Also, I was well aware of just how much it would compromise my status as an objective researcher were I even to begin to hint at such a possibility.

No – the truth was that I saw this as a wonderful opportunity for an experiment. I could now go through the process that so many before me had experienced. I could seek the star child that might be hiding inside.

I hoped that by doing this, and if I could retain my objectivity, then I might have an advantage. For I would know first hand what it was like to piece these things together in your mind and that would help when judging the stories of others.

In truth, I really did believe that I would discover how the human mind plays tricks upon itself and relishes making something out of nothing. I expected that my temple of strange phenomena would fall about my ears as soon as I dug deeply into the truth behind these dreams.

I chose Dr John Dale as my guide. He was a clinical psychologist who specialized in handling phobias. He knew a little about the UFO subject, had hypnotically regressed one woman to her abduction and concluded that it was some kind of fantasy. I knew that he was not going to try to talk me into something strange because he believed in it himself.

I would walk the two miles to see him week after week, because I needed the time to clear my head after each session. It was a very odd experience in itself, almost like going through deep psychoanalysis.

At first we talked generally about the mind, memory processes and the use of regression hypnosis. Then we tried a few relaxation exercises. Eventually we built this into a strategy of recall.

I had agreed up front not to try to check out any details that might be available to affirm any memories of these events. I had notes, diary entries and other records available. But these would provide a really useful cross-check after the experiment was over upon which we could then judge the effectiveness of regression hypnosis memory.

When we were ready, Dr Dale asked me to tell him what I thought were the key events to be explored. By now I was used to relaxing and free to say what I really felt. He warned me that I had to learn to tap into the subconscious and recognize when it was confabulating. He told me that it was common for a surface memory to act as a cover for a second layer in which the mind gave the subconscious what it wanted to hear. Only when you peeled away that layer of onion skin might the real truth emerge.

Whilst we talked generally about many things, it was to the Chester experience that I was continually drawn. This was a surprise. It was not what I would have predicted, because I really believed this object was just an aircraft. I actually wanted to revisit Blackpool, or the New York train.

The first session simply allowed me to visualize and describe the night in question. We used it to draw out some facts – such as the date, the day of the week, time of night and also extra information. For instance Dr Dale asked me why I was in Chester, when I had arrived, when I went home, what I had done earlier that day, and so forth. I knew there was a reasonable chance of finding out much of this information even though I had consciously forgotten it. Indeed that proved to be the case.

When I checked back I found that a lot of the information that I offered under hypnosis was inaccurate. I would say 50% of it was found to be wrong. For example, I reported the correct date (3 August 1977) but said it was a weekend. It was in fact a Wednesday. I also gave the time as 9.30 p.m. when I could later establish it was really 10.45 p.m. On the other hand, I got some things right that seem unlikely to have been mere guesswork – such as the number of days I stayed in Chester. It should be stressed here that I visited the city often, for different lengths of time. Recalling the details of any specific trip more than a decade later is consciously impossible.

As the hypnosis proceeded I was intrigued that it was not like what I had expected it to be. I did not fall asleep or forget everything that was said to me. It was merely a state of relaxation where images popped into my mind like I was watching a movie. I relayed the action to both Dr Dale and my own conscious mind. At first this was done in the past tense e.g. 'We had been to a pub by the river that day.' Eventually, it just became routine to describe the action as if it were unfolding there and then e.g. 'There are five swans on the river. Paul is throwing something at them.'

By the end this visualization was strong, but never at any point could I be sure of the source of the imagery. It formed a continuation with what I know are true memories, but the pictures that appeared could be memory or they might just be imagination. I was never emotively involved in such a vivid way that I could insist without question that what I saw was reality.

Dr Dale told me that complete absorption within the storyline is rare and only occurs with the best hypnotic subjects – those possessed of great visual creativity, I would suspect. Most of the time subjects simply talked themselves into assuming that what they saw was real, because that is what they had come to the hypnosis session wanting to believe.

I suspect that a hypnotized subject in a UFO situation will feel even more pressure to acknowledge the truth of these images. After all, they have come here because they want hypnosis to plug a gap in their conscious recall. Around them are researchers who may have invested time and money in the clinical procedure. There are several incentives that must motivate the person towards coming up with the goods and accepting the images as real.

All I can tell you is that, so far as I was concerned, I saw images from somewhere and it was all truly fascinating, but there is no way I can be certain that they were real memories. This is particularly true in view of the fact that some of the checkable 'facts' were clearly offered incorrectly.

I could prove that the events had not occurred on a Saturday, as I insisted under hypnosis. Equally, I could prove I was in Chester for three days, just as I had correctly told the psychologist when he asked. But if a witness suddenly reveals that they have been inside a spaceship no amount of checking through diaries and calendars is ever going to tell you if that piece of data is one of the 50% that is recalled as fact or the 50% that is inaccurate fantasy. Hypnosis testimony seems to produce both.

What I did find was that memories directly related to the UFO incident were actually stronger and more likely to be accurate than general memories surrounding the sighting in the Chester field. Later I discussed this with a psychologist at MIT who specialized in hypnotic memory and he told me that the UFO event was itself a 'memory hook'. Onto this many directly relevant details were pinned by the subconscious mind and so locked into place. As such these were easier to retrieve under hypnosis than were unrelated incidents which the mind had less reason to record.

So what did I describe under hypnosis about that fateful night in August 1977?

Here is a record of what took place, with the reminder that you should tread carefully when interpreting its meaning.

Paul and I left the pub (at which I had drunk no alcohol at all – as I almost never do). We walked through the field and sat by the fence looking at the clear and not completely darkened sky. I could feel the damp grass touching me.

Then the light appeared – vivid blue in colour, shockingly so. It came at us from the railway line, dropping to rooftop height.

> We're on the field now ... Paul to the left. I'm to the right. The blue light is just coming. It's steady. Not pulsating. I say, 'That's a funny aeroplane,' and Paul looks at it for a minute and says, 'It's not an aircraft it's a UFO.' He's laughing. 'Yeah,' I say. 'This is exactly the position that people are in when they think they've seen a UFO ... But (aah ...) Why is there no sound? Why is it silent?' He's not laughing quite so much now. He's now saying, it's an aeroplane and I'm saying, no it's not!
>
> Why has it come here? (aah ...) There's nothing to see. No lights to guide it ... Now there's a searchlight coming

out. It's shining down ... (aah ...) It's lighting up the ground ... Oval ... It's not an aeroplane.

Paul is static ... Now it doesn't look like an aeroplane at all. There's a dome on it. A vertical beam. There's a ... a ... figure in the dome. I can only see it dimly ... (aah ...) I know the figure. They know me. But this isn't for Paul ... It's a check up. One of many. But this one's important because of what's happened ... Paul ... It's the timing of it ... They want to know what's going on with Paul ... Why?

There's a pulling sensation ... tugging ... sucking up ... They say 'Hello again' ... but in my mind. I can't see them properly ... but the head is ... not big, but not small ... About five feet. Only one of them takes any notice. The others ignore me ... He's holding something in his hand ... like an egg ... going up and down ... saying, 'This is recording information. You don't need to know ... not yet.'

Now we are running away ... I have hold of Paul's arm. I'm dragging him up. Fifteen minutes has gone but we don't know. Paul doesn't even realize that anything has happened ... aah ...

As I was also told, things would pop into my mind over the next few days. I should record these and watch my dreams carefully. Extra information could emerge that way. Indeed it did. Almost as many new images appeared – e.g. when I was washing up – than had come out directly via the hypnosis.

One thing that I was reminded of was a postscript to the Chester experience. This was undeniably real and recorded at the time. It happened about twenty hours later at my home back in Irlam. I was still away in Chester.

My mother had heard a humming noise filling the room. She looked around the bungalow but could find no cause. A few minutes later she was outside talking with a neighbour when they both heard the noise again. They looked all around them but did not think to look upward into the sky. Then there was a sudden pop – like a loud baloon bursting – and all was calm again.

Moments later the neighbour's children came up and pointed to the sky. They – and, it later transpired, another person passing nearby – had seen an oval object in the sky the same colour as a sodium street-lamp. It had been the source of the hum and had hovered on the moss immediately adjacent to our house at about rooftop height. The explosion coincided with the object having instantly disappeared.

Superficially this sounds like ball lightning. But there was no thunderstorm. Nor was it raining. It seems to have been preceded by the humming noise inside the house, and the way it homed in on our bungalow is curious. Indeed, it was in almost the same spot where the following April I saw the orange light that I then dismissed as a helicopter crop spraying.

The coincidence of this unusual event occurring at my home in my absence within hours of the sighting back in Chester seems noteworthy.

More obscurely, I 'learnt' through dreams and flashbacks in the wake of my hypnosis that there had been several other visits during my life. The Chester incident was significant for them because I had only met Paul a month before and they were puzzled by our relationship.

I saw further details of the entities – with slit-like eyes and very white skin. Their mouths gave the impression of a permanent smile when you looked at them closely. I had never heard that said before by any witness.

I was told that I was being used as a communicator of information. Many others were performing similar tasks. Most did not know of this. They also explained about the genetic experiment. In effect they were attempting to change the world by stealth. By spacenapping millions and making small genetic alterations to the human gene structure they were trying to make us less aggressive and more like themselves. They hoped that this would work its way through the human reproductive chain. Then they could stop the experiments and nature would take its course. They could afford to wait a hundred years if necessary, but thought it would not take that long.

Whether this is sheer imagination or true revelation, who can say? All I know is that it was fascinating to undergo.

11   The Star Child Mystery

We have now examined some of the evidence concerning the star child mystery. Most of this has been anecdotal, relying upon the testimony of individuals alone. Any law court will tell you that this is a dangerous practice, which is why criminal convictions rarely depend upon eye-witness statements. They always seek harder, more scientific, analysis.

I could not attempt to persuade you that this exists in great abundance for the claims of spacenapping victims. Quite obviously it does not, otherwise there would be no controversy over the star child philosophy.

Quite properly you will not have been convinced by all of these stories. In your circumstances, I would surely not be. They represent fantastic accounts about what is an even more fantastic phenomenon and should never be accepted merely because some people believe them to be true.

There are three basic ways to evaluate this mystery, but I will rule out a fourth – which many of you may feel is the most plausible of all. That view is that there is no case to answer, every one of these accounts is an invention – hoaxes created for the sake of fame, fortune or more obscure reasons.

I can never prove that all the stories in this book are not made up. I would not be surprised if one or two of them are. However, from all that I have seen about the way this phenomenon affects people's lives and the intense lack of desire most witnesses have to talk about it in public, I would frankly be amazed if that were always the case. I strongly believe that many of them are believed to be the truth by the people who report them.

In any event, I have good grounds for dispensing with the 'all a hoax' conclusion. Whatever the truth about any other case, I know that my own experiences happened just as I say they did. So this ,fact is inevitably good enough for me to need something more when seeking an explanation.

The three main possibilities that we will assess in the concluding chapters are that there is a psychological, metaphysical or extraterrestrial interpretation to resolve the star child mystery. I have no burning need to prove any one above the other. Frankly, like you, I am just keen to learn the truth and eager that to do so we must explore all the available options. All I would ask you to remember, particularly if you are a hard-headed sceptic, is that viewing every option includes real alien visitors just as much as it includes some form of hallucination or delusion. I know that is tough to accept. It took me quite a while to embrace the possibility.

However, before we move on to look at what these potential solutions have to offer, it will be useful here to take some time out. We can then summarize what the star child theory actually is, at least according to the mass of testimony that we have faced up to so far.

Firstly, it proposes that an alien intelligence – from some source – is here on earth and in contact with humanity. Indeed, by all accounts, that it has been so for a very long time. Quite possibly that means the entire conscious history of the human race. Alien need not mean another star system; although that is the origin most frequently proposed by contactees and spacenap victims alike. In truth it simply means a non-human intelligence of at least our equal (and apparently more than our equal) which is able to interact with us on a regular basis, regardless of whether it comes from alpha centauri or some source that science has not quite figured out yet – e.g. a parallel reality, or some inter-penetrating dimension.

However, there is more to it than just one intelligence coming here. All the reports point very firmly towards two quite specific types of alien being with different and yet extraordinarily consistent features. In terms of evidence that something is going on, the lack of variety and the indisputable patterns that recur from case to case must rank as about the strongest clue. It is difficult – though not impossible – not to see this as proof that witnesses are perceiving real entities.

The two types of entities are best summarized as follows.

There are the tall ones. These are usually of above average height – six to seven feet not being uncommon. They are thin, but relatively human in appearance. They could be – and indeed are often said to be – living on earth undetected. They are described as possessing blond hair, pale faces, often blue eyes with vaguely oriental features. Witnesses have spoken about their resemblance to Greek athletes or ancient gods. The term 'Nordics', because of their resemblance, in part, to the Scandinavian race has also been applied by UFOlogists.

Moreover, the behaviour of these entities is as consistent as their appearance. They are reported to be relatively friendly and helpful – or at least not openly hostile. They often answer questions and spout a good deal of philosophy or issue warnings about the future. Yet most remarkable of all is that they are possessed of magical powers. They do not seem to need spaceships and frequently materialize and dematerialize, pass through walls and windows and communicate invariably with the witness by telepathy. In every respect they act as if they are extremely gifted psychics.

Whenever the two entity types are together (as they almost always are in modern cases with medical experiments aboard a UFO) it is the tall ones who seem to have the upper hand. They use the other beings as their agents. Indeed cases are known where the tall ones even warn about the less friendly ways of these other visitors.

The second alien type is very different, although also basically humanoid. They are definitely smaller than the human average. Three and a half to four and a half feet is common, but heights up to just over five feet have been recorded. They could not pass for humans in the streets, possessed as they are with grey/white or even bluish skins, hairless heads that seem disproportionately large, huge dark eyes and underdeveloped mouths. The term 'greys' has been adopted, particularly by American UFOlogists.

These small entities are clearly less friendly. They rarely say much to humans. They seem to behave like scientists performing laboratory experiments on a lower species of life – not going out of their way to cause pain, but as if the task is more important than the way that it gets done. These medical experiments seem to be their field, but often with one of the taller entities watching in the background and in control.

The small entities seem to be more closely tied to the UFOs than do the tall ones. There is much less evidence of psychic powers. They are said to be emotionless, humourless and occasionally have been mistaken for robots or mechanical creatures as a result. In some cases witnesses have been told that they are a biological machine – a sort of working android – engineered by the tall aliens to perform menial tasks.

Despite this, most books about UFOs still carry the claim that these 'greys' are the real visitors, perhaps simply because they are the ones in most direct contact with the witnesses by virtue of their job.

You may have noticed that these two types of being fit closely with two obvious mythological creatures. The Nordics are the equivalent of Biblical angels and the epitome of master magicians. In the same way the greys are both demonic and, mythologically speaking, akin to trolls or elves. Since all of these entities are widespread throughout human belief systems in nearly every culture on earth then they must signify something important.

Is it that these two types of entity fulfil some kind of psychological need deep within ourselves? Are they perhaps a sociological reflection of good and evil or higher consciousness and the subconscious? Or, perhaps, these religious beliefs and the mythological stories are all reflections of dim historical awareness that we have always been in touch with two kinds of real supernatural entity. The modern version – extraterrestrial visitors called Nordics and greys – may be no more than a space-age version again misinterpreting this fantastic relationship.

Be they real or metaphorical, these visitors are engaged in two specific tasks on earth, according to what the evidence tells us. These are calling people to act as messengers and also genetically engineering some part of humanity. Both result in what we call star children.

According to some witnesses, aliens claim to have seeded star children on earth for many millennia and say that great religious figures were alien representatives. I have heard from some sources (including contactees and spacenap victims as well as government figures on both sides of the Atlantic) that this is the true reason for the official cover-up of UFO evidence. Admitting the reality of aliens is no big deal, but coping with religious turmoil would be a nightmare if it were made public that aliens claim to have manipulated most major systems of belief. No government wants to take responsibility for the revelation that religion is an alien P.R. exercise.

The purpose of these alien 'representatives on earth' has been to try to raise humanity up the ladder of evolution without resorting to direct intervention. It is said that we have been observed since we were primitive tribes and our progress charted, almost like we might plant a rose garden and try to produce the ever more perfect rose through generation after generation. In a way this makes the aliens seem like a substitute for God; although that is not what they claim to be. However, the fear that their presence here would be perceived this way is what supposedly causes those 'in the know' to refrain from telling the world about this mystery.

After these infrequent visitations scattered throughout history, the alien programme reputedly went through a dramatic change in the wake of the Second World War and, particularly, from the mid-1950s onward. Indeed, the genetic engineering experiment can trace its clearest origins to within days of the Russians first sending a life-form into the earth's orbit aboard Sputnik during October 1957. This date, in the context of the history of the planet, will probably be far more important than any war or political upheaval that took place during the rest of the twentieth century.

Some feel that our sudden ability to explode nuclear weapons and destroy the earth, and, more recently our ecological efforts to speed towards catastrophe, coupled with this new-found ability to export our mistakes to the rest of the universe with the space programme, meant that the alien's long-term plan had to be stepped up. It is undeniable that there was a major transformation in the alien contact evidence precisely at this time – which is either highly significant or a big coincidence.

The first wave of messengers during the 1950s were the contactees, who founded many cults and semi-religious associations. These groups adopted an alien theme – being in communication with 'wise masters' and 'space brothers' who were passing on pleadings that we should mend our wicked ways. This was to pay considerable dividends during the next couple of decades thanks to the large followings that these cults attracted, particularly in the American west. They laid the foundations for the new age movement that blossomed afterward. This, in a slightly different way, speaks today to the same kind of people with very similar messages.

But the problem with contactees was their messianic zeal. They went on lecture tours, wrote books, even stood for US president! Non-believers thus suspected (perhaps wrongly) that it was all self-deception or fraud.

Coincident with the demise of the contactee movement, during the late fifties a completely new type of messenger emerged. People began to discover that during chunks of time inexplicably missing from their recall they had been spacenapped – usually by the taller entities. During these events, assuming that we accept as truth the memories that plug these time lapses, victims were implanted with information deep into their subconscious mind. Knowledge of a specific task was programmed into them. Few people are aware of what that task is – often being told that they will know when the time is right, when prearranged signals are to be released all at once around the world. However, some feel that they have been encouraged to act as missionaries to spread the alien word. They do so, not by forming cults or promoting themselves, but by a much more gradual communication process.

After a handful of contactees were urged to make maximum impact via the creation of major cults we now have a far more subtle process. Thousands of people, perhaps more, are being contacted day by day and then implanted with tasks to perform at some appropriate moment. Many of these are helping to spread the word now. Others may not stir into action until the right moment is upon them, whenever that is.

It is a weird concept – almost like a planetful of pre-programmed zombies instilled with post-hypnotic commands to obey an unseen and unknown alien master plan.

Put like that it all sounds pretty horrific. But according to the evidence the purpose is more gentle than it seems. I have heard the term 'education programme' used and it does appear to be less a case of indoctrination and more one of enlightenment. The end result, supposedly, is the future benefit of mankind.

These people are, in a sense, all star children. But rather more disconcerting are the claims about the renewed alien plan to seed actual physical representatives on earth.

There is some sign that in the 1940s and early 1950s attempts were made to adapt the genetic structure of human babies whilst still foetuses in their mothers' womb. Parents were told that their child would be 'special' and would somehow belong to an alien race, whilst strictly speaking born as a human.

This is a scene chillingly similar to Mary and Joseph in Nazareth being told by an angel that they would bear a son and call him Jesus ...

How well this initial programme worked is hard to tell. Some of these star children now claim to have memories of this event. Others are possessed of great psychic powers. For instance, at least one medium, one famous healer and one of the world's best-known psychics profess some alien intervention in their early life. There could well be many others.

Who knows how many of these people are in influential positions, perhaps in the ecology or peace movements, or even in government? Who knows how many are not yet aware of this intervention in their youth? It is certainly also worth noting that people born in the late forties and early fifties reached maturity during the era when the peace and hippy culture flourished in the sixties and paranormal phenomena attracted great attention around the world.

However, regardless of the success of this modest start at genetic tampering, from the late 1950s onward there were clear signs of a more direct and extensive process. Men and women were seemingly selected, repeatedly spacenapped and monitored, then eventually samples were extracted and a full-scale genetic experiment was mounted upon their DNA.

By all accounts what this involves is the use of human sperm and ova which are extracted from chosen victims, mixed together and then tinkered with by alien technicians and finally reimplanted into the womb of a female abductee. When the child, thus conceived as an alien/human hybrid, is perhaps a foetus of only three or four months, it is removed and brought to maturity by artificial means in the alien environment.

What happens next is less clear. Are any of these hybrids brought back to earth to grow here? Or are they still out there somewhere waiting to restock the planet following some imminent great disaster? This coming 'sequence of events' frequently alluded to during abductions and spacenappings, seems to be the driving purpose behind this genetic experiment.

Some human men and women have therefore been used as pawns in a grand plan. Because of the way that they have been selected they may feel special or part of the star child programme. They may even feel protected.

Yet the most direct form of star child, if Ruth Montgomery and some witnesses met in this book are to be believed, is the actual replacement of a human spirit by some sort of alien consciousness – an extraterrestrial possession where the person literally becomes a star child.

As we have seen there are cases where humans allege such an origin. We may well want to refer to these people as mentally ill. Yet they seem to survive throughout their lives without exhibiting other signs of delusion. It is as if the only thing wrong with them is this quite ludicrous belief.

Of course, one question that may well have occurred is this. If it is possible to 'take over' a human body by ejecting the tenant's 'soul', with an alien spirit moving in, then evidently these entities have no obvious need of a physical body. Why then do they waste time on very physical medical experiments – and, indeed, why do they need spaceships at all?

Of course, if this whole thing is a psychological process then it need not follow logic at all. But possibly there is another, more spiritual, explanation. What if the aliens are real, but their spaceships do not exist? They could be images constructed to help us accept the idea that these visitors are from another planet, when in truth they co-exist side by side with us on earth.

Or, again, if these craft are real they may be created as an environment for human beings – somewhere to take us when the medical experiments are needed. Perhaps we only think of them as spaceships for these entities to fly around in because that is what we want to believe for our own peace of mind. In truth these places are laboratories into which they place us – created just to meet our physical needs.

Imagine that a marine biologist was interested in a dolphin. The scientist might render the animal unconscious as it swam curiously towards a searchlight on a boat. Then, with the dolphin unaware of what had happened, it could be taken back to a specially-created tank that was purpose-built to house dolphins in some nearby seaport laboratory. Surrounded by strange dials and equipment the scientist may then plant an electronic tagging device into the still groggy creature, then give it another shot to render it unconscious for the fretful journey home and, taking it back out to sea, replace the captive into its own environment.

Dolphins are intelligent creatures. We know they have a language and social structure. What would our seanapped dolphin tell its peers? No doubt tall tales about this big light that approached, how suddenly it awoke in a strange craft shaped like a water tank and surrounded by dials. How here was this strange bipedal monster prodding and poking about. Then, inexplicably, the dolphin was back in the sea and hours had suddenly disappeared ... Pull the other one, fellow dolphins would surely reply.

The point is that, here, the dolphin would interpret the water tank and laboratory equipment as part of the 'alien spaceship' that it was zapped aboard. In truth it would never have been conscious of the real mode of transportation – the marine biologist's boat – and what it thought of as a craft was a stationary unit that had been designed just to accommodate dolphins whilst the tests were carried out. Sceptical dolphins would no doubt point out that this weird alien's 'ship' was a bit too dolphin-like, complete with a watery environment. If these creatures did not live in water but outside it then why was their ship full of water?

And why was the scientist doing these tests? Not to hurt the dolphin but to learn more about it and, we might argue, to ultimately benefit the dolphin race by using our advanced technology to assist them.

This analogy is not as silly as it sounds. It may be the closest we can come to tracing what goes on during a spacenapping. As the poor dolphin's experience clearly shows, many of the things that look to us to be illogical may not be illogical from the alien perspective. Equally, some of the things which we consider part of the alien environment may, in fact, be really part of an environment that they have constructed just for us.

That people believe they may be star children seems undeniable. That many more claim to be victims of an alien master plan is even more obvious from examination of the data. That there has to be some reason why this is all happening at such a prodigious rate today is surely self-evident.

The only thing we need to know is what form the ultimate explanation will take. Are we right to believe that we are not alone in the cosmos and that forces beyond us are meddling with the earth? If so, then we need to know as much as we possibly can about what they are up to.

But first we must tackle the real prospect that all that looks alien may be far more down to earth. That the answers to the riddles are to be found not in outer space but within the still uncharted realms of inner space and the human mind ... the final frontier which even Captain Kirk has never conquered.

12   All in the Mind?

In 1992, Derrel Sims, a hypnotist and investigator with the Houston UFO Network, came up with a fascinating plan to research spacenappings. Half a dozen witnesses who alleged lifelong contact were given a suggestion by him under deep hypnosis. The idea was to convey this to their alien captors during a future visitation and establish some kind of direct link with the investigation team.

In November 1992 one of the Texas abductees supposedly had a further spacenapping and fought against the mind control of the small grey entities. Just before she succumbed to this powerful medium she screamed out, in recollection of her hypnotic suggestion, 'We know what you are doing ... we know all about you!'

Within a few days several other hypnotized subjects claimed to have been abducted again. From subsequent hypnosis sessions on five of them – reputedly done independently of one another so the witnesses could not share details of their memories – an extraordinary sequence emerged. Three of the five claimed to have been abducted on the same night – 8 December 1992 – and to awake with conscious memories of nasal bleedings on the bedclothes.

These witnesses all described basically similar experiences; although with important differences. One thought that she was dead and that her deceased brother was standing nearby, another that she had been transported to heaven and was within the presence of God. A couple of others interpreted the events more obviously, as being inside a UFO.

Despite these differences, all of the subjects reported

being in a similar-looking meeting-room where they were interrogated by entities that they knew from before. A typical case was of a man who related what had happened to him as follows.

He had been woken by a brilliant flash of light (like lightning without thunder). A small grey entity was then visible in his room and he was led outside to a blue spotlight beam shining onto the ground. The next thing he recalled was being inside the large circular room, just as reported by the other abductees in apparently very similar fashion.

The subject was then confronted, not by the greys, but by a much more human-looking individual whom he had never met before. This being asked how the man knew about his previous abductions. He was then shown a model of the human brain and asked to identify the subconscious mind. Of course, the witness was incapable of doing that. Eventually he became aware of other humans in the room, all naked as he was himself. They were being probed in a similar way, apparently unaware of the presence of other spacenap victims within their midst.

The abductee finally reported that a debate broke out between two of the taller, human-like beings as to whether their 'experiment' could continue now that their victims had some form of control over the situation. They blamed the greys and, it seemed, the greys were not exactly enthralled by the techniques being used by the tall ones either!

This is all fascinating stuff for a variety of reasons. It shows, not for the first time, that there can be a dynamic interaction between the abductee and the abductor. The familiar scenario here is of countless victims taking part in an experiment with two different types of entity that seemingly adopt their own stances and methodology.

In that sense, the case seems to offer support for the pattern that keeps emerging and implies that these experiences may be real. Yet, what of this curious reference to the subconscious mind? Is that an image that is meant to convey something, just as a dream can be filled with symbolism which a psychologist can decode to learn much about our mental welfare? Indeed, is the fact that a post-hypnotic suggestion can adapt the flavour of the spacenapping some sign that it is, in essence, just a psychological phenomenon and directed by what goes on within the mind of the abductee?

I recall a case where the witness, a young girl, was frightened of the aliens' return. I suggested she keep a camera in her room as 'aliens do not like to be photographed'. This fib kept them at bay for weeks. When she next had an experience they told her, 'We did not come because of the camera.'

In other cases where I have been involved a similar process has surfaced from time to time. I recall one poorly executed hypnosis session where a witness reported a scene and explained that aliens rose from one level to another within their UFO. It was then implied, innocently but clearly by the hypnotherapist, that this seemed hard to understand. Did they not have some way of getting from floor to floor, like we do by using escalators? Almost in the next sentence the regressed witness was describing escalators inside the UFO – something that, so far as I know, has never been recorded in any cases before or since.

We have also noticed how some pieces of information from previous accounts can find their way into witness testimony during an altered state of consciousness. Remember the way in which aliens smelling of cinnamon only seem to have cropped up after Whitley Strieber first described this effect in his own case?

In the Alan Godfrey abduction, the witness plucked out of the air the name 'Yosef' for the alien and said that it was wearing a form of skullcap. This is an unusual and Biblical-sounding image. Presumably within his subconscious mind Alan was aware that some of those interested in his case were of the Jewish faith (where the cap symbolism fitted neatly) and quite possibly even that the doctor in charge of the hypnosis was called Joseph. Did the abductee unconsciously adopt this information into his story?

I know that when I was 'regressed' to a past life during

an experiment, I later found it fascinating that the name I gave for my prior self – which, as with Alan Godfrey, just tumbled into my head – came forth as Mary Reynolds. Only later did I realize the significance of this. I had forgotten (but probably did know unconsciously) that Mary Reynolds was a real life Rip Van Winkle, who had experienced a long-term time-lapse during the nineteenth century. Also note that Reynolds is not an entirely dissimilar name to my own. Mary was also the name of the hypnotherapist!

Indeed, in a later part of the session I gave another name – Alan Dale – and only discovered some weeks later that there was an Alandale Road just around the corner from a house that I was then about to move into. I had visited the new area once, so almost certainly passed the Alandale Road signpost, but I had no conscious memory of that fact. Had it surfaced under hypnosis as the stimulus for a fantasy? Does this occur more than we think?

This process is well known to psychologists and is called cryptomnesia.

Another weird episode had occurred during the Aveley, Essex, abduction. I attended one of the hypnosis sessions on Sue, the mother of the family, carried out by parapsychologist Andy Collins. In the midst of my asking questions of the hypnotized subject something curious happened. She gave an answer which, I suddenly realized, was being offered as if conveyed directly to me by the aliens. So I proceeded with more questions and found that, for a short time, I could use the hypnotized witness as if she were a telephone and I was speaking, through her, on a sort of hotline to the tall, blue-eyed entities that had spacenapped her family four years earlier.

Nothing spectacular emerged in terms of information from this session, but I tried it again during a couple of other hypnosis experiments with abductees. Once it worked, the other time it did not. Yet, realistically, how could you communicate at all with these alien entities during regression hypnosis unless you were actually speaking – not with a separate intelligence out there somewhere – but with a part of the subconscious mind of the abductees themselves?

Think back also to Alan's story in chapter two, where he

later realized that he had unconsciously adapted the memory of his spacenapping over time to the point where it more nearly resembled other stories that he had read.

Then, in 1993, British researcher John Spencer conducted some experiments with willing volunteers where a hypnotherapist used post-hypnotic suggestion to drill into them a memory of a fictitious abduction experience. After several sessions most of them could spontaneously describe this as if it had really occurred. The problem was, of course, that it had not. The experiment was video-recorded at various stages and this proved to the 'witnesses' that what they presumed to be an actual recollection was merely a false memory instilled under hypnosis.

This same technique has been applied in non-UFO situations. In one case a woman was interviewed about a night during which nothing odd had occurred and she slept soundly. Through hypnosis she was persuaded that she had actually heard a gunshot. When now asked about the same night after these sessions, she 'recalled' the gunshot as fact and was amazed when it was proven to her that this memory was a hypnotically induced illusion.

All this evidence, plus the discovery that 50% of normal hypnotic testimony is proven to be bogus and presumably just fantasy, explains why hypnosis is not used extensively to aid witnesses in courts of law.

Equally, I have to say that when given the chance to be honest and not put under pressure by expectations of success, witnesses do tend to say that they cannot guarantee the objectivity of abduction memories produced under hypnosis.

Police officer Alan Godfrey was one of the first to be brave enough to admit this, pointing out that whilst he is absolutely sure that he did see a real UFO in Todmorden during November 1980 he cannot be as positive about the 'on board' adventure that he described under hypnosis the following summer. In the intervening weeks he had read UFO books and knows that he could have unconsciously incorporated data found in these. All that he can do is to report how the images that came into his mind seemed lifelike – but confess that this is not the same thing as asserting their reality.

However, hypnosis is not the reason why we have alien contact stories. Throughout this book we have come across many cases where it has never been used at all. Indeed, prior to 1987 about 40% of spacenapping stories did not depend upon regression; although that has fallen to about 25% now that the technique has become so widespread in the USA. Yet there is no evidence to support the view that memories produced under hypnosis are different from those where this technique is never applied. Even so it should be remembered that in cases when hypnosis is not the source of the spacenapping account, some form of altered state of consciousness – e.g. vivid dreams – often is.

It also cannot be disputed that hypnosis can stimulate actual memory of events buried in the subconscious to about the same extent that it can trigger some kind of fantasy. So, whilst we must accept that hypnotic testimony is suspect, we can never forget that it really might sometimes be the key that unlocks that hidden door to truth within the mind.

In fact, everything we know about the way in which hypnosis operates tells us that in regression back to a UFO situation our memory is more likely to function well than in a non-UFO situation. The meaning and import of the experience boost the percentage of factual memory to above 50% and reduce the level of fantasy to somewhere below that. Indeed, the philosophy of using regression hypnosis depends upon the well-known rule that hypnosis is more likely to be accurate if the context of the experience is replayed. Thus, taking a person back over the mental surroundings of their experience can help.

It is worth noting that the same effect can occur – without using hypnosis – simply by taking the person physically back to the location of the encounter and asking them to 'walk through' the experience on site. Experiments have shown that this technique, which I have used once or twice as a substitute for hypnosis and call 'creative visualization', is as helpful as any regression might be. It also overcomes any doubts that the use of the hypnotic method is sure to bring about.

Similarly, whilst it might seem attractive to assume from experiments like those conducted by John Spencer that people can fantasize quite realistic abductions, it is not quite as simple in practice.

A previous experiment, which Spencer's was emulating and extending, was conducted by Alvin Lawson, a California English professor, with the help of a hypnotherapist, Dr William McCall. They hypnotized eight students screened for lack of knowledge of, or interest in, UFOs. The group were then asked to invent an abduction. Some superficial similarities were found with real cases, but in truth there were far more differences. A range of entity types were described, for instance, none of which were common in real data.

I reproduced the Lawson/McCall experiment myself – using creative visualization rather than hypnosis and with two sets of ten people. Group one were UFO naive, like those in the California test. Group two were not and had read, experienced, or even investigated UFOs; although none were abductees or contactees to the best of our knowledge.

There were marked differences in the results. The UFO-aware people described abduction-like scenarios – with familiar entities and techniques. The UFO-naive people did not. Not a single one of those subjects invented the greys or Nordics, medical examinations or genetic engineering claims. In addition, none reported the 'doorway amnesia' syndrome and quite a few of them vividly described the point of entry into the UFO – e.g. being 'beamed up', led up a ramp by a ray gun, and so forth. The differences between these stories and the real spacenapping claims could not have been more obvious.

In fact, in all of these experiments there is one critical omission that never appears in the fantasies and yet almost always features in spontaneous claims of spacenapping – the emotional impact of the episode. This involves both the intense fear and, paradoxically, the sadness upon departure of the entities.

As you can see, we have points that favour and some that do not support the contention that this subject is basically psychological in origin. However, we can certainly isolate some factors about the witnesses themselves. These are the clues that three decades of research have shown to form the typical background of a potential star child.

They tend to be of above average intelligence and to display an unusual level of interest in space or the cosmos. Other pursuits frequently take them into the realms of mystical, new age studies and ecological or peace campaigning. Indeed, there may be a specific turning point in their lives where this took on prominence for no obvious reason.

These people also tend to be very quick as children, often described as being advanced, i.e. reading and talking at an unusually early age. Indeed they may be looked upon as strange as a consequence or be referred to as an 'old head on young shoulders'. Also they tend to be emotional and to often enter caring pursuits e.g. more nurses than any other profession are found.

Coupled with this is the ability to remember very early periods of life. The average adult cannot recall anything before the age of about three and only scattered memories between three and five years old, but star children are quite different. They can typically recall scenes whilst in their crib or pram – perhaps when just a few weeks or months old. Some even claim memories of their own birth.

As these children grow they adopt a life profile of strange phenomena. The UFO and abduction stories are but a part of many other things that happen to them – starting with the psychic toy light balls that appear in their bedroom and including a range of psychic phenomena – notably, out-of-body experiences, precognition and, less often, psychokinesis or poltergeist effects around the house. Their dream life is also vivid, with floating or flying unusually common and lucidity within the dream state beyond the normal level.

Also you find that these people grow to adopt artistic talents of some sort. This often shows most obviously in their handwriting, which tends to be filled with curls and ornate detail. More specifically they will write poetry or stories, paint pictures or pursue some other type of artistic hobby that involves their powerful visual creativity, such as pottery.

As you see, we have learnt a great deal about what kind of person is likely to be a star child, even if we do not yet know why this happens.

In 1993 a detailed review of what UFO witnesses are like was published in the *American Journal of Abnormal Psychology*. It was compiled by a team of researchers: Nicholas Spanos, Patricia Cross, Kirby Dickson and Susan DuBreuil.

In effect they looked at two samples totalling forty-nine people; those who merely saw UFOs and those who had alien contacts. The second, whilst not necessarily all star children, are closely akin to the kind of people we are concerned with. Two comparison samples of 127 individuals – being students and average citizens (none of whom professed any UFO experiences) – were also studied with the same huge battery of standard psychological tests. These were designed to analyse all sorts of life profile information.

The most important finding was that there was not the slightest evidence to support the theory that witnesses – even those who claimed the most bizarre experiences – were pathological, disturbed or suffering from any unusual psychological traits. The most notable positive discovery was that those who had claimed weird experiences tended to possess more exotic belief systems e.g. in alien life or survival of death.

Of course, this cuts two ways. Whilst, in effect, it establishes, as have several other similar tests, that there is no support for the view that star children are suffering from psychological delusions, it does not explain which way around we should consider the correlation that was discovered between exotic beliefs and strange experiences.

For instance, it may mean that people who believe in various strange things are more likely to experience them. Or indeed, that, unlike others, they may interpret odd happenings within their life as being supernatural rather than natural.

On the other hand, it may well also fit the evidence uncovered in this book that such people have a lifelong profile of strange phenomena. Inevitably, if you encounter odd lights, experience out-of-body sensations and floating dreams, or see aliens on a frequent basis from babyhood, then it stands to reason that you are going to grow up believing in these things as real. Whereas others, who never experience the phenomena, or not with any such regularity at least, are obviously not going to develop the same kind of belief systems and will instead adopt the sceptical society view.

Which comes first – the belief or the experience that appears and supports the belief?

A brave attempt to find an acceptable psychological answer to this whole confusing mystery was presented by psychologist Dr David Hufford. His intriguing book, *The Terror That Comes by Night* – published more than a decade ago – assessed the 'old hag' phenomenon in Canadian culture. This is, in effect, a claimed nocturnal contact with an often invisible spirit presence which appears in the bedroom and directly interacts with the witness e.g. by crushing sensations on the body. It is obviously similar to the age-old phenomenon of the incubus or succubus, which in mythology is said to be a spirit of the dead that returns to rape both male and female victims in the middle of the night.

Hufford later saw the parallels with spacenapping cases and, more recently, the growing star child beliefs and reported on his views at MIT. He noted how his research during 1985 in Newfoundland studied 254 people and discovered nocturnal accounts of paralysis, a presence in the room and a pressure on the body in between 14 and 17% of cases (with added, but less common, features of a tingling sensation and a buzzing sound). These are remarkably similar symptoms to those often related by abductees – indeed the 1992 Roper Poll of potential abductees (the biggest ever survey in the USA) discovered an almost identical percentage (18 as opposed to 17%) for the belief that an entity was present within the bedroom.

Hufford insists he is not a sceptic and has anomalous cases difficult to fit into a straightforward scenario. But it is inescapable that the same type of data that his witnesses in Newfoundland were reporting and then fitting into the popular legend of the old hag is, elsewhere, being adopted by witnesses as evidence that a person is about to be spacenapped.

Perhaps the physical and mental sensations are globally consistent and only the cultural interpretation of what they mean changes. Is that why abductions were viewed as demonic or as trips into fairyland in past centuries, when we had no modern belief in aliens? Is it also why some modern cultures – e.g. the vast Indian sub-continent – seem oddly bereft of alien contact claims? Is there a different cultural niche into which these people slot the same experiences and symptoms? In support of this Cynthia Hind found that in Africa natives rarely report their alien contacts because, even today, they regard them as visitations from ancestral spirits.

The question is – which of these evaluations of the physical data is accurate? Must our western view of alien contact be the correct interpretation?

Dr Eddie Bullard, a folklorist at the University of Indiana, has extended Hufford's plea for inter-disciplinary research into the field of abductions. He has compiled the most comprehensive database of spacenappings and applied all the standard rules of mythology to these stories. He first did so in 1986, convinced he would establish that these reports followed the normal folk-tale pattern so that he could then show his colleagues that UFOlogy offered them space-age folklore in the making.

As it was to turn out quite the reverse was true. Every test Bullard did upon the data came up blank. These cases simply did not follow the rules of folklore in any way. The evidence behaved as if it were a real phenomenon – being reported with frightening consistency. After studying over 800 cases the folklorist is convinced that, whatever is going on, this is not mythology but is something that is really happening; although he is far from sure what that something is. However, he appears not to reject the possibility that it is what it seems to be – real alien contact.

One problem I think we have to bear in mind is that the folklore with which researchers are familiar tends to come from a time when stories were more often handed down by word of mouth months or even years after they had first happened. The spacenapping affair is bound to be different, because today we talk to witnesses within days or even hours of their encounter taking place, and, more significantly, the huge media explosion – via books, tabloid newspapers, movies and TV – distributes a common account of what reputedly occurs to a worldwide audience with extreme rapidity.

The ground rules have changed since medieval folk in isolated villages told of their encounters with the fairy folk. They did not have the chance to go on *The Oprah Winfrey Show* and tell the world all about it, or, indeed, sell the rights in their story to the *Daily Star* and its millions of readers and then do a deal with Steven Spielberg to make a movie seen by countless people around the globe. If they had would the result have been fairy lore that quickly became just as consistent as modern-day abductions? We probably cannot answer that question, but it must never be overlooked.

Dr Rima Laibow is a New York state psychiatrist who has taken a deep interest in what she calls 'experienced anomalous traumas'. This allows her to pay special attention to the potential relationship between child abuse and spacenappings.

Dr Laibow, in a fascinating piece for the *International UFO Reporter* (May 1989), describes how in her patients she has found that victims of abduction often profess child abuse in their early life. As a result the theory developed that perhaps the alien contact, especially given its abusive content, was a cover story invented by the mind to try to deflect attention from the truth – that the abusers were, in fact, family members.

In a series of case histories the psychiatrist cogently argues why this seems unlikely. Most problematic is the fact that victims of child abuse tend to repel the memory and invent screens that remove the anxiety in some way. The creation of a substrata of recall in which the full horror of the experience remains intact is an unlikely screen to adopt. Moreover, the nature of spacenappings is such that the trauma seems, if anything, greater and the purpose of hiding a terrible incident with something that *feels* real and is more horrible still seems very obscure.

The correlation that does exist could have a number of explanations, according to various experiments that have been carried out by child abuse specialists. In fact, up to 40% of women and 16% of men appear to have had some experience of abuse within their early family life. Such surprisingly high statistics indicate that the number of abused spacenap victims may only seem significant because the true population of abuse victims within 'normal' society is generally underestimated.

Of course, the child abuse memory may act as a screen against the more horrific alien abuse. In one case reported by a psychiatrist, when the 'truth' emerged under hypnosis and the patient 'realized' he was not being abused by his mother but by little aliens his mental health improved drastically. He could not blame her for this unavoidable alien attack. But if this was a helpful screen why was it not the surface memory all the time?

Recent studies of children alleging satanic ritual abuse, notably in Britain during the late 1980s and early 1990s, found almost no evidence to mount prosecutions. Yet so sincere had been the claims of these children that their stories were treated seriously and, in some cases, they were taken from their families and put into care. What if their memories of being sexually abused by strange masked figures were real but had been sublimated as ritual abuse by humans? No evidence of this would appear – because no human abuse took place. Who in authority would even contemplate the possibility of an alien source for the real claims by these children?

Another consideration is PTSD, or post traumatic stress disorder. Victims of major disasters, e.g. plane crashes, suffer from it, as do those who have been raped or abused. It has a very specific set of symptoms and most abductees indisputably show them.

By itself, all this establishes is that spacenap victims believe in the reality of their trauma, not that this trauma actually occurred. But PTSD from events that are only imaginary is fairly rare and contentious.

American psychologist Brenda Dean has noted how in PTSD sufferers two forces are strongest. One of these is the need to transform the terrible experience into something positive, which we see with kidnap victims who often emerge from the trauma viewing their captors in a favourable light. Perhaps that is relevant to the new age, ecological and spiritual changes that some abductees display after the event.

The other force is the need to blame someone, anyone, and not to allow their suffering to be the result of just 'one of those things'. This might cause victims of an unknown psychological phenomenon that is triggering assorted forms of abuse – e.g. the old hag, incubus, satanic rituals and now spacenapping – to find someone, somewhere to be considered responsible. Perhaps the aliens are just the latest in a long line of scapegoats adopted by the human mind.

As you may have realized by now, far from UFOlogy being full of spaced-out nutters sitting on hilltops waiting for the latest shuttle from Venus to fly by, it actually has a rich subculture that is seriously endeavouring to find working solutions to what goes on. Whilst the sceptics usually just debunk without thought and wish the mystery away as 'obviously delusional', much of the real effort to get to the truth comes from within the phenomenon itself.

Of course, there are wide-eyed believers who will not truck anything but aliens from the stars and huge government cover-ups. But equally there are psychologists, sociologists, physical scientists and objective UFOlogists who enjoin a debate in sources such as the exceptional *BAE* (*Bulletin of Anomalous Experience*). This sadly leaves most of the critics looking bereft and as pathetic as a dyed-in-the-wool, don't bother me with the facts, type of believer.

In a 1992 issue of *BAE*, for example, Texas UFOlogist Dennis Stacy came up with an original theory, which was then debated at length by colleagues during the next year. The feasibility of his concept, which personally I and many of his critics find slim, is less important than the fact that it was created by a UFOlogist and argued vigorously and sensibly by other UFOlogists – whilst predictably being ignored by mainstream science or the debunkers who tend to regard all UFO buffs as daft.

Stacy proposed that the genetic experiment/alien hybrid

syndrome may be a psychological drama expressing the current public debate about the abortion issue. He referred to the round eyes and large head of the entities – i.e. the foetus-like characteristics (one abductee had even described the aliens as looking like an 'overgrown foetus'). He wondered if somehow this powerful motif within present-day society was stamping itself upon the pre-existent abduction mystery and trying to impress a point through vividly realistic images that were being acted out within the mind.

It is an interesting theory, mirroring one brought to the fore by Dr Alvin Lawson, the professor whose imaginary abductee experiments we referred to earlier in this chapter. Lawson had proposed that abduction memories were accounts of the trauma of birth bubbling to the surface. The medical examinations, probes, lights and so forth offered a degree of tacit support.

Sadly, the so-called birth trauma theory failed as all good theories should by virtue that it allowed empirical results to be predicted. If it applied then the imagery which should emerge via normal birth should not apply to cases where the witness was born by Caesarean section – a quite different surgical procedure. And, of course, vice versa. However, no such differences were apparent within the data, suggesting strongly that the birth trauma theory was a brave try but was ultimately not correct.

I suspect the same end will come to the abortion debate hypothesis. One of its major problems seems to be that alien abductions are reported by children – who, I suspect, are too young at the ages of seven or eight, for which some reliable cases are known, to be aware of – let alone powerfully care about – the controversy over the rights and wrongs of abortion.

Even so, it is this kind of search for a working hypothesis which the subject needs. We must explore every option and I greatly applaud Dennis Stacy's desire to think laterally around the issues.

The strongest contender for an explanation has in recent years been the fantasy prone personality (or FPP) hypothesis. This was designed in the early 1980s by psychologists Rhue and Barber in a completely non-UFO context. It has been most vociferously promoted within UFOlogy by Australian care worker Keith Basterfield, and psychologist Dr Robert Bartholomew.

In 1990 a few of us were very optimistic that this theory might provide an answer of sorts. That optimism has not totally evaporated, but it is beginning to wear rather thin. Indeed, after the debate at MIT, Keith Basterfield publicly withdrew the theory from the arena; although I feel from recent correspondence that he is still trying to find a way that might take this data into account.

What Rhue and Barber had discovered was simple enough. They had isolated a group of individuals within society whom they termed 'fantasy prone'. An exact figure is difficult to give as everyone is to some extent fantasy prone and it really depends what point on a sliding scale you choose to regard as being atypical. However, in general you might say that about 5% of the population were vividly fantasy prone.

In truth what this meant was that these individuals had such a rich fantasy life that they often found it difficult to distinguish reality from imagination. Their dreams, for instance, were so vivid that they tended to wake from them wondering if they had been real. Finally day to day life took hold and they asserted control upon their inner selves.

Furthermore, FPP sufferers (if that is the right word as many found it a pleasurable ability) experienced odd phenomena throughout life that we would term supernatural – out-of-body sensations, flying dreams, etc. They were also vividly creative, with more than average numbers of 'imaginary friends' as a child (some persisting into adulthood), and took seriously some experiences that most of us would dismiss as imagination.

One problem that has to be remembered here is that to some extent this depends upon who defines what is real. Our consciousness is a continuum between real and imaginary and in truth everything that we perceive is a product of our brain decoding and interpreting signals that come in. We dictate by consensus which of these things we allocate to 'the real world' and which we call 'imagination'. But we have no proof that we are right.

It may be that fantasy prone people can experience things that most of us cannot and we dismiss the reality of such perceptions purely because there are fewer gifted with FPP than the rest of our blinkered selves. Being in the majority, what we say is what tends to be considered real.

Therefore, merely saying that abductees are also FPPs is not necessarily the solution to the mystery.

In any case, a number of experiments have been conducted and all have failed to demonstrate that there are more FPPs amongst a sample of abductees than there are to be found amongst the general population. This is a major surprise, as quite a few of us were confident that there would be clear evidence for this. The overlap in psychological traits seems strong.

More work is being done as, so far, all studies have been based in the USA and there is a real need for cross-cultural surveys. However, at the moment nobody is getting carried away with anticipation that the FPP theory will provide the best way forward.

It is worth noting, however, that FPPs often experience what are termed hypnagogic and hypnopompic imagery – visions on the borderline between wakefulness and sleep. These are hallucinations (that is, so as not to belittle them, what we can define as images generated within the mind which have no visible external stimulus). They can be so strong that they are considered real by the person concerned.

London psychiatrist Dr Morton Schatzman wrote of his research into an American woman in his fascinating book *The Story of Ruth*. She had such vivid hallucinatory experiences in which she saw her father behaving just like a ghost. Only he was not a ghost, because whilst she was seeing him in London he was thousands of miles away still living in the USA. Eventually Dr Schatzman helped Ruth control these images and she could conjure up visions to order. They were so powerful that they followed physical laws.

In one test, carried out by neurologist Dr Peter Fenwick, the 'ghost' was made to stand in front of flashing lights. If this passed through to the retina then Ruth's brain must respond. It could not fail to do so, even if she claimed to see the apparition blocking them out. As nobody else could see the apparition then it could not *really* be there and Ruth should still see the lights. She did not. Her brain responded exactly as if her apparition were standing in front of the lights blocking their path to her brain.

I myself have experienced a hypnagogic image and discussed it with a psychologist at the West of England University, Dr Sue Blackmore.

It happened one winter's morning in early 1979 when my boyfriend had set off for work. It was cold and icy outside and I was worried about him travelling on his motorcycle. A few minutes after he left I saw him come back. I got up from the settee by the fire and expressed my relief at his return. Then I woke up. For, despite the fact that this was an all-senses, completely realistic vision, it evidently had never happened.

I must have dozed off because the fire was stifling the air and had this vivid hallucination of my boyfriend's return, presumably thanks to my intense desire that he should come back. Everything that I lived through for a few seconds was indistinguishable from real life. I only know that it never 'really' happened because I 'came to' and found myself still on the settee and my boyfriend not there. Later I could confirm – by asking him – that he had never returned that morning; although he did tell me that he nearly changed his mind when he saw the state of the country roads. Did I somehow tune into his indecision as to whether to turn back?

Of course, as I told Dr Blackmore, I knew this was an hallucination because I could test it against reality. But what if instead of my boyfriend in his riding leathers I had seen my dead grandmother, or, indeed, a little grey alien materializing in that room. When I came to on the settee they would have obviously gone, just as my boyfriend had done, but I would have had no way to check afterwards if either of these beings had ever been present. I am virtually certain that had this occurred I would now be insisting with so much conviction that I could pass a lie detector test that I had once seen my grandmother's ghost or had my own living-room alien contact. I would believe it without a moment's hesitation.

Dr Blackmore could only agree with this diagnosis and suggest that in this way many seemingly real and very vivid close encounters might come about. The term for this psychological phenomenon is 'false awakening'.

In a sense this ties in with the latest field of research within the realms of psychology; false memory syndrome (FMS). Whilst, again, it was never postulated as a solution to the spacenapping mystery, UFOlogists have been quick to seize upon the possibility that it just might be relevant. Others have been just as quick to use it to debunk that solution.

In fact, it emerged largely from the worrying discoveries that children who professed satanic ritual abuse, or child abuse by family members, had, in fact, apparently suffered no such abuse at all. Yet they clearly believed they had, just as I was briefly certain that my boyfriend had come home.

We have, in fact, suggested that in some of these cases the abuse memories might be a cover for an alien contact of some sort. However, psychologists have naturally not considered that view and developed the hypothesis that the memory is false and has just become accepted as truth by the patient, possibly as a consequence of the therapy carried out upon them. In other words, the trawl through their past life searching for meaning behind phobias had seemingly uncovered a child abuse memory as the source, but that was in truth just the invention of the mind (perhaps during regressive hypnosis).

It was further speculated that during the course of repetitive hypnosis and therapy, and because of the need to come up with some source for their problems, the patient (and their doctor) accepted the false memory as truth – sometimes with devastating consequences (e.g. unfounded allegations by the police against family members). Legal action against practising therapists has become a real threat via patients who develop FMS during treatment.

The fact that a truly believed-in memory could turn out to be utterly false and be made worse by (even created as a result of) the investigative process rapidly opened up the spectre of its application to strange phenomena – notably alien abductions. How many spacenap victims were being manufactured as a consequence of FMS and the passion for using regressive hypnosis in case after case?

Dr David Gotlib, a Toronto psychiatrist and editor of the *BAE*, has reported throughout 1993 and 1994 on the legal actions, the clinical diagnoses and the intense controversy within the psychological press about the reality or otherwise of FMS. As he reports, the one thing both sides of the argument frequently cite to support their case is that under hypnosis people can 'recall' a spacenapping. Since alien abductions are considered impossible by virtually all practitioners their existence – indeed explosion in numbers – is used as proof. Either it is seen by one side of the fence as evidence that FMS in valid and important areas (e.g. child abuse) really can operate or by the other side as an illustration of the desperate lengths that disbelievers in FMS will go to, associating such a 'trivial' thing as aliens with important social issues.

In fact, of course, the reality or not of alien abductions is central to the whole question of FMS. The dismissal of it from all consideration by most sections of humanity is more worrying than its entry into the FMS debate. For, whatever else is true, there can be no doubt that people do believe in the reality of these experiences and are undergoing frightening life traumas as a result. These are every bit as deserving of due consideration as are claims of satanic ritual abuse. The problem is that UFOs are a scientific taboo, however sensibly you study them.

All we can say at this early stage of the FMS/ spacenapping argument is that it offers some likelihood that the uncontrolled research within the UFO field is responsible for the fabrication of some believed-in memories of abduction events that never took place. The day cannot be far away when someone suffers as a result (e.g. tries to commit suicide because of fear of alien kidnap) and a distraught relative blames the unqualified UFO buff who has practised amateur hypnosis in their burning quest for the 'story'.

Indeed, whilst the sceptics have given them not one iota of credit for the fact, British researchers foresaw this problem long ago. In 1982 I travelled the country securing views from UFOlogists to create a 'code of practice' to govern interaction with witnesses. The hypnosis clause was soon tightened up and insists that only medically qualified practitioners can use it in the UK. The code was then made mandatory for all members of BUFORA (the British UFO Research Association) – despite considerable opposition in some quarters where it was viewed as meddling and irrelevant.

I put the code as an appendix into the back of my 1986 book *Science and the UFOs* – the one that Strieber read which helped bring him into the UFO field. Sadly nobody seems to have picked up on it and not a single source in the USA has ever adopted it to my knowledge. Indeed only the Australian Centre for UFO Studies was brave enough to follow BUFORA's lead and agree such a set of principles controlling their investigators. As a result, I fear, many UFO groups and amateur researchers are heading for a fall and the ones who will really suffer will be the witnesses.

In 1987, still not happy, I pushed a move through the BUFORA investigation team to impose a voluntary moratorium banning the use of regression hypnosis in UK cases. This was meant to send a signal to the UFO world. Nobody outside Britain responded. In 1993, when forced from my post as investigation coordinator, it still operated. I doubt it will in future.

Of course, just because FMS might create some abduction claim out of nowhere is not to say that no abduction claim, even those largely emerging via hypnotic regression, is ever genuine. Even proponents of FMS are not suggesting that no real child abuse ever happens just because false memories of it are possible. Exactly the same comment applies to abductions.

As Dr Rima Laibow notes, 'the event level, nuts and bolts, hypothesis [i.e. that alien contact is real] is, I am afraid, the best hypothesis we are able to build out of our current state of knowledge.' She adds that she understands how hard it is to accommodate this weird idea, despite the fact that it fits the data better than any present psychological theory seems to do. So, she is quite right to point out; 'it is prudent to continue to search for other hypotheses which do less violence to our notions of the cosmos'.

That search continues, but as yet it has not been successful.

13   A Spiritual Revolution?

One problem within the quest for truth about the star child concept is often overlooked. We largely predetermine what we are seeking by setting out our theory in advance. As such it is hardly too surprising that we discover evidence that matches this idea and ignore all that which does not.

What I mean here is this. If we assume that we are looking for cases where people claim contact with aliens (i.e. by popular translation, extraterrestrials) or, reports from people who believe that they themselves might have an alien origin, then we instantly limit the scope of any possible solution.

True, we might find a psychological cause for the evidence that emerges. As you have just seen the search for this solution within inner space goes on. But the only real alternative would otherwise be to accept the literal truth of what these witnesses profess – alien kidnap.

However, it has to be possible that there is a 'real' phenomenon taking place which is simply being misinterpreted by most witnesses and investigators alike – that they see it in terms of alien visitors, but the truth is more complex than that. If so, then we will only grasp the possibility by widening our net and taking into account data that die-hard extraterrestrialists will reject as irrelevant – if, that is, they even bother to give it a moment's thought at all.

I have in the past often written about possible natural phenomena that might induce changes in the brain that stimulate vividly real experiences. In that sense the 'UFO' would exist, as an exotic natural process which science has yet to come to terms with, and the more bizarre alien component would depend upon as yet undefined psychological processes.

This option is the subject of considerable research, e.g. by Canadian neurophysiologist Dr Michael Persinger, and remains, for me, a valid idea. I will not discuss it here as you can find much about it in my earlier books.

Yet there is a further option to take into account which, to date, has had scant attention; although that is thankfully beginning to change. This really stems from one of the most obvious patterns in the star child data which, until now, most extraterrestrialists have run away from. Why is there such a high preponderance of psychic phenomena interspersed between the alien contacts? It is as if the spacenapping is no more than one element in a lifelong process but has been exaggerated in importance by our decision to lay the blame for all of this at the feet of alien intruders.

The prospect that looms large is that the alien phase is but a feature of a broader range of star child symptoms which, taken together, point towards a more metaphysical conclusion. Perhaps the reason why star children seem to be obsessed with these matters and appear to go through a spiritual evolution during their experience is because that is the real point of what is happening to them. It is as if we have been trying to see what the weather is like by looking through a keyhole into the back yard, spying one tiny spot on the ground and noticing that it is dry. This might tell us that it is not raining but adds nothing about whether it is warm or cold, windy or calm, humid or arid, and so forth. In other words, it tells us very little.

To use a more contentious analogy, few scholars who are objective would suggest that the only way to seek out spiritual enlightenment about the nature of God would be to read the first page of the Bible and base all your conclusions on that. At the very least they would say read the rest of the 1000 pages of text and, if they are truly honest, admit that valid insights can also be gained by studying the teachings of Buddhism, Islam, and many other religions.

Yet we seem to be adopting the same blinkered process.

We are basing our opinions on just the alien abduction and paying no attention to the broader span of life experiences reported by these witnesses. We must take a more holistic approach to what is going on.

Fortunately, some researchers have woken up to that fact and are beginning to explore the exciting possibilities. Bill Chalker in Australia, for instance, has long recognized the value of researching aboriginal beliefs centred around the shaman. Most tribal societies have such wise folk (sometimes termed the medicine 'man' – although they can be women too). I suspect mediums and star children are Western society's shamans.

The shaman is regarded as a conduit between our reality and a spiritual dimension where other wise intelligences dwell. These people have visions, psychic experiences, vivid dreams and 'alien contacts'. They appear to be exactly the folk we would call fantasy prone, or candidate star children, depending upon our view-point. The main difference is that they are treated with respect within their society and regarded as the font of true knowledge that makes them leaders to be followed. We treat our shamans like misguided idiots and I suspect we are all the poorer for it.

We might be missing out on key parts of the star child mystery by focusing too intently on its alien contact stories. As an illustration we need only see the undeniable overlap with the NDE – or Near Death Experience.

The NDE is a phenomenon that has been known for centuries but which was first studied in detail with the publication of Dr Raymond Moody's 1975 book *Life After Life*. Since then many psychologists and medical doctors have researched and written about it and countless books have appeared. In 1994 one NDE witness – Betty Eadie – had her personal account top the US best-seller lists for weeks on end such is the cultural impact of these claims.

In simple terms an NDE occurs when a person comes close to death – e.g. during a sudden accident or surgery in hospital. Since in some such cases no drugs were administered whilst in others anaesthetics were applied you can see that it cannot be an artificially induced phenomenon, otherwise it would only be found in situations when a person was under medical treatment.

The witness often reports floating out of the body, seeing themselves down below but free of all pain. Then a bright light appears and a cone or tube emerges from it. They float along this and may meet strange beings who communicate with them by telepathy. They are finally returned back magically and find themselves where they were – trapped under a car and fighting for breath, being rescued after almost drowning or recovering from the anaesthetic with relieved surgeons glad to have dragged them back to life.

Given improved medical techniques and our ability to snatch folk back from the brink of death you can see why the popular interpretation of this now very well-documented phenomenon is that these people have headed towards an afterlife and then returned to earth. But you probably spotted the obvious similarities with cases of alien abduction.

Only a few UFO researchers saw the parallels, largely, I suspect, because of the narrow-mindedness rejecting anything not patently extraterrestrial.

I wrote several articles on the theme in the magazine *Exploring the Supernatural* during the mid 1980s. Later, Peter Hough and I tried to get psychologist Dr John Shaw, then at Manchester University, to research the patterns and he put us on to leading UK researcher into NDEs, psychologist Dr Margot Grey. Neither seem to have responded to our challenge, sadly. However, eventually Dr Kenneth Ring, a psychologist at the University of Connecticut, did see signs of the importance and contacted me. He and I subsequently had some interesting correspondence. Ring worked on what he called 'the Omega project' – later to become the title of his 1992 book that published all the statistical results of this in-depth analysis.

What Ring and I were both noticing is twofold. Firstly, there is a clear link to be found in the experience. A UFO witness experiences the Oz Factor, sees a bright light and a beam or tube associated with it, feels a floating sensation and then is suddenly inside a strange place where they commune with human-like intelligence. In an NDE more or less the same thing takes place but is interpreted very differently.

However, in addition, as Dr Ring was finding, those who experienced NDEs were emerging from them with a positive and spiritual view of life, often exhibiting artistic talent and experiencing all sorts of psychic happenings. That, of course, was just what star children were describing.

Some examples of the parallels will rapidly make the point. Bear in mind that when a UFO context was placed upon these events by the witness a quite different evaluation could just as easily have been applied. The story would then probably have been ignored by 99% of UFO researchers.

Graham from Lancashire heard a faint buzzing noise in bed late at night. He then became paralysed and lost all sensation. A huge light poured down from above and exploded all around him and he found himself inexplicably inside a strange room with light oozing around him from no obvious source. He was located by a long table, or bed. Suddenly his recently deceased father appeared and spoke into his mind that Graham must return. A light appeared and Graham tried to enter it, but was forced back. He was dropped down in a beam, saw his house from above and 'came to' in bed.

John had experienced psychic phenomena and UFO encounters investigated by Margaret Fry. He entered hospital in Cardiff on 17 November 1987 for hip replacement surgery. As he was wheeled into the theatre under pre-op anaesthetic, still conscious, he began to rise from his body and was able to watch the operation. During the rest of the time he was in the presence of a tall human-like being who told him 'we are rectifying things wrong with your body'. He later heard the surgeon say to others in the theatre, 'It's amazing, this man has healed himself' (although, apparently, the hip joint still needed replacing). Before he left hospital one of the nurses admitted to John that she and a student nurse had seen his image rise up out of his body and return later. However, on his return only the top half of his body had been visible. The legs and hips were missing! The two nurses were terrified that he had died, but he was clearly still alive. Indeed, during the early stages of the surgery John had babbled on under the anaesthetic about aliens. The doctor, assuming he was recalling an earlier experience, even asked John to describe his 'odd dreams' during a later ward round.

Reg, from Leeds, was feeling very tired one day in February 1976 and lay on his bed. There was a sudden pressure on his body and two tall beings with pasty faces and cat-like eyes materialized in his room. They talked to him by telepathy and urged him to stretch out prone and they would take him. As he did so Reg drifted up through the ceiling and saw a UFO hovering over the roof. The next thing he knew he was inside a room on a long table or bed with the beings using an eye-like device to scan his body. Reg was then told odd things and that he was being sent back. He found himself on his bed, struggling for breath and paralysed for some minutes.

Gaynor, then a young child, was also in bed in 1979 in her Deeside, North Wales, home when she saw a light above her head. A tube emerged from it and she was sucked upwards, feeling like a speck of dust drawn into a vacuum cleaner. The next thing she knew she was in a strange garden (children's NDEs often involve gardens for some reason). Two human-like entities with cat's eyes and pale skin who were just over five feet tall were with her. After being shown various images she was sent back. Her mother entered the room during this 'experience' and was scared. Her daughter was rigid and prone on the bed as if dead; although soon after, on her return, all was well again.

Jim, a professional magician in Middlesbrough in 1964, was undergoing oral surgery in the dentist's chair when he suddenly found himself out of his body and drifting upward through the ceiling. Above the surgery was a UFO and he found himself inside, standing beside a tall human in a white robe who poured information directly into his subconscious mind using telepathy. Jim was informed that a great disaster awaited the world and he had to return to warn people of this. However, to do so he would have to fight off small, evil beings trying to possess his body. He forced himself back to just above himself, sensing other presences around him, and saw the dentist struggling to revive him. In what seemed like desperation the dentist hit Jim hard on the chest, and yelled out 'Hit the road, Jack!' – the title of a then popular tune. Instantly Jim was back in his body recovering from this brush with death. The dentist confirmed that the patient had abreacted to the anaesthetic and he thought that Jim was in real trouble for a moment or two.

We could go on, but these five cases from my files make the point well enough. None of them are straightforward spacenappings. All have clear elements that fit the NDE. How you interpret them is a personal thing, but they imply that the two phenomena may be much more closely related than we suspect.

In at least three of these cases the witnesses had a track record of strange phenomena during their lives. In at least two they emerged with a very positive outlook on life thanks to the experience – taking up what might be termed metaphysical pursuits and interests.

We might think that these cases occurred close to death. Some aspects of Reg's story, for instance, could imply that he suffered a mild heart attack without realizing it and both John and Jim were obviously in near death situations at the time. Yet that seems improbable in other cases and, besides which, one of the most important recent findings in NDE research is that they occur at times other than when the person is close to death.

Psychologist Dr Sue Blackmore, probably the most forthright sceptic of the 'trip to heaven' theory for NDEs, has found a few of these cases in her work. It is one cornerstone of her 'dying brain hypothesis' as featured in her 1993 book Dying To Live.

Dr Blackmore cites an example of a climber who fell from a mountainside and crashed hundreds of feet into soft snow. He got up and walked away almost unscathed. During the fall he underwent numerous symptoms of the NDE e.g. the out-of-body sensation and another common feature, that of seeing many images flashing before the eyes (which seems interestingly akin to the abductee tale of aliens sprinkling data 'like hundreds and thousands', as one witness phrased it, throughout their mind). Yet, as the man's survival shows, his body was never in imminent physical danger of death during this fall – although, in cases like this, the person may suffer near fatality through shock.

Dr Blackmore contends that these people merely believed that they were about to die and that was enough. This triggered the body's defences into operation – pumping chemicals into the brain to deaden pain and setting up other processes that she believes are built into the human body computer to 'ease the passing'. These – as side effects – induce the out-of-body state and other psychological illusions.

Of course, the fact that NDE-like symptoms appear to occur in abduction encounters is a point that Sue Blackmore would no doubt argue strengthens her theory. They too, she will say, are products of the body trauma and the witness has just placed a different context (alien contact instead of visit to an afterlife) around the mental experience, possibly because they did not think, unlike most NDE victims, that they were in imminent danger of death. Instead they had assumed they were being spacenapped by aliens.

Perhaps what counts is the initial evaluation placed upon the first stimulus e.g. the out-of-body sensation, unusual light or floating sensation. If the witness judges that they are dying then an NDE may be read into the physical and psychological symptoms that follow. If the person feels that these are all indications of an alien landing, then a spacenapping may result. Possibly in the past, when neither NDE nor spacenapping had been invented as options by our culture, this experience would be given another context, a trip to fairyland perhaps or an incubus attack. This might explain what we found earlier; that such things have always happened throughout history but have been perceived differently.

Perhaps in this light we can evaluate other cases in this book rather differently. What of the man rescued from drowning in New Jersey by an alien guardian (page 83)? Or, indeed, those others who profess some kind of spiritual salvation as the starting point of their star child memories – such as the boy who was catapulted off his bicycle and believed that he was rescued as he lay in a coma (page 58)? Were these near death experiences that were interpreted in an unusual manner?

Dr Kenneth Ring's statistical analysis over several years established beyond any reasonable doubt that there is more than a superficial link between these disparate phenomena. He conducted major psychological life profiles on both NDE survivors and alien abductees and found that they were very similar. But together they differed from his control sample of non-abductee or NDE witnesses. The profile uncovered was pretty much the one we isolated earlier in this book, i.e. visually creative individuals.

Just about the only thing that altered between NDE and abductee survivors was that the former had a much greater belief in an afterlife and the latter in extraterrestrial intelligences. What we sadly do not know is whether these different beliefs arose because of how each person evaluated their experienced symptoms, or whether a pre-existing belief in heaven or ET dictated the form that the context of the experience followed.

However, whilst many UFO researchers applaud Ring's Omega experiment and are intrigued by its results they have been less than enthusiastic about the manner in which he interprets what he has found. Dr Eddie Bullard presented Ring's data in his absence to the MIT symposium and made clear that he had told his colleague that he'd do his best but could not publicly support the conclusion that Ring had reached.

So what was this shocking conclusion? A clue can be found in his title – *The Omega Project*. Omega is the final letter in the Greek alphabet – and is, therefore, a symbol of the ultimate.

It may be very relevant to recall the phrase which Reg

from Leeds says the aliens offered to him during his experience outlined above. This, if you remember, was an exact duplicate of what Gary, the self-professed alien, had uttered to me on the telephone only days before Reg had his abduction. Both men had referred to the term 'I am the alpha and omega' (i.e. the beginning and the end).

Interestingly, Jim claims that the aliens he met above the dental surgery had also explained to him that life was a circle (i.e. without beginning or end) and he had to help humanity break free of that chain.

No doubt, given this, you may have spotted the delicious irony of the name of the one scientist who seems to sense the parallels between the NDE and spacenapping experience. *Ring* could hardly be more appropriate, could it!

Ken Ring feels, rightly or wrongly, that we do not need to make a choice between imagination and reality when we try to interpret the NDE or spacenapping. He feels that these things occur in a third realm – which he calls the imaginal – a sort of spiritual dimension that few of us get the chance to experience, except maybe on rare occasions.

Once, he says, we were all more in tune – and, perhaps, shamans today are still touching this other place. The metaphysics of this imaginal reality are what one finds in most deep or esoteric teachings throughout the world, i.e. it is both life and death, real and unreal, timeless and eternal, and so forth. In effect, you might say, it *is* both the alpha and omega. Within this imaginal world the mind is enhanced and all powerful – what we want to be real *is* real.

It has similarities with my concept of the waking lucid dream state outlined in my book *Sixth Sense* (Robert Hale, 1988). I argued that this was a previously unrecognized niche on the spectrum of reality and a kind of mirror image of the lucid dream. In the well-attested lucid dream state the dream world of imagination is moulded and shaped by the mind, which is conscious of where it is and what it is doing. I am lucky to have had lucid dreams (as have about one in five people). They are fantastic adventures.

In a waking lucid dream state the mind would still be

dominant but the scenery that is moulded and shaped would not be imaginary – it would be real.

Perhaps the two concepts come together in Ring's imaginal realm, which is where all these fantastic things take place.

He also feels that the sudden explosion of these phenomena in the recent past is like a global near death. I would rather phrase it that our human consciousness may be undergoing a spiritual revolution – perhaps passing through a metaphysical puberty. Possibly the various images of imminent catastrophe found during spacenappings are symbolic images about this transformation rather than the literal reality that witnesses fear.

Ring sees NDE and abductee alike as forerunners of a future breed of humanity – prototype new age people. Their enhanced ESP, spiritual views and visionary encounters with other life-forms are more than just meaningless personal hallucinations – as sceptics contend – but are equally a lot more than just meetings with men from Mars. Profound as this event seems, in truth it would be of limited consequence to us as human beings. Instead, Ring feels, these visions are the growing pains of a new and better human – a kind of super person (or Omega person as he would call them).

As you no doubt realize, Omega people and star children are just two names for the same essential concept. Indeed, if a great deal of what we are experiencing is allegorical – as it seems to be – then confusing aspects of the star child story suddenly begin to make sense.

Naturally, star children will think of themselves as 'alien' to this world – for that, in a sense, is what they are. Of course, they will regard themselves as missionaries – for, again, that is the role they are sent to play. They will miss the imaginal realm when contact is lost – for they feel at home there. The values they adopt are those that seem important to this new breed of human now in embryo – indeed, the image of genetic experiments by higher entities using selected people to build a new and better race suddenly takes on symbolic beauty. These visions of alien experiments are expressing exactly that image of birth and regeneration of the human race.

If Ring is correct in his judgement, we should stop fussing about the literal truth of the alien medical experiments or seeking proof that hybrid babies are really being born. New humans are springing up in great abundance – star children are even now taking over the world by stealth. But they are speaking the language that all mystics have used – from Jesus to Buddha to the modern-day abductee. They express a metaphysical truth in glorious pictorial imagery. Spacenappings are the parables of the 1990s.

We should seek the meaning underneath these false illusions and recognize that it does not matter if witness A has not 'really' been inside an alien spaceship and then been sent home with a genuine precognition to change the world. Forget the spaceships, put the aliens on hold and concentrate on the message that lies beneath this verbal candy floss.

Yes, something wonderful might well be happening, but does it matter how concrete that something is? Listen to your mind, not your brain. Follow your soul, not the instruction book of sceptical logic. Then you may wake up.

14   Cosmic Citizens

Dr Leo Sprinkle is a fascinating man: a counselling psychologist, UFO researcher, new age pioneer and, by all accounts, a star child.

In 1968 he was contacted by the University of Colorado, who then had a massive government contract to investigate UFOs. The infamous Condon Report (named after team leader and atom bomb physicist, Dr Edward Condon) was the result. It was to prove a watershed in UFO study.

The Condon team wanted Sprinkle to offer psychological evaluations about a police officer from Ashland, Nebraska, who in December 1967 claimed to have met a UFO which siphoned power from overhead electricity lines in the dead of night. The officer made a matter-of-fact report on what had happened and Sprinkle was very pleased to assist in the search for truth.

This witness, Herb Schirmer, proved a straightforward, upright citizen. Everyone backed him – his friends, neighbours, his police chief. Sprinkle could not find a thing wrong with his mental health, despite the team conducting what was by then the largest ever group of psychology tests on a witness. The patrolman himself requested a polygraph test and sailed through it without a flicker, indicating that he undoubtedly believed in the truth of what he saying.

At this time the hypnosis experiments on Betty and Barney Hill were fresh in the mind and Sprinkle decided to regress the highway patrolman. As a result a now typical (but then near unique) spacenap by pasty-faced Nordics emerged in which, amongst much else, the entities had told Schirmer about their current attempts to analyse options for the carrying out of human 'breeding' tests.

When this was put on record it seemed like the most absurd nonsense, but today it slots quite perfectly into place.

The police officer was not claiming that these experiments were happening. Like the few other witnesses who then added a piece to the jigsaw he was referring to an alien 'analysis' of this scheme. The experiment itself seems to have largely come afterwards – in a neat, orderly sequence that surely would not have emerged if these tales were nothing more than random hallucinations or personal fantasies from wayward individuals.

Not surprisingly, Schirmer got a clean bill of health from Dr Sprinkle.

Of course, the Condon scientists did not see it that way. They wasted two years investigating at great expense only sixty cases and failed to explain about one third of these, often with incredibly positive conclusions. These noted how in one case all the facts suggested a real UFO was involved, or how, in another account, they suspected the UFO was an unknown phenomenon so rare it had never been reported before. And so on. Lights in the sky or dubious photographs were given reams of assessment in the half a million word report. Schirmer's case got two pages and the entire spacenapping testimony that came as a result of their study was not even discussed and dismissed glibly in a mere four words: 'new information was added'!

On the surface the university report seemed pretty conclusive hard evidence of UFO reality, which was liberally scattered throughout the book (indeed the project requested – and got – more money to extend their research, hardly suggesting they were finding nothing much). But Condon's overall conclusion was that UFOs were a great big waste of time.

Schirmer's case was one of the two-thirds that Condon did not term 'unexplained'. The reason for this was not, however, that the scientists had successfully explained it.

They simply chickened out, arguing that there was no physical evidence to back it up, ergo it could not be regarded as scientific proof of anything.

In fact, there was some physical evidence – a metallic fragment found at the site. However, as they could not conclusively link it with the UFO, and (although they never said this) because, I suspect, the trooper's story was just too wild for them to take seriously, they effectively ignored this solid data after nothing beyond a cursory glance.

This is how science first came head to head with the star child mystery – and the US taxpayer was the one who footed the bill.

Fortunately, Dr Leo Sprinkle was not so easily fobbed off. He became ensnared by this entire phenomenon. Thirty years on Sprinkle has probably regressed and researched more victims of spacenapping than anyone else in the world – heading for 350 at latest count.

His views about this are utterly fascinating , because he takes a very different approach from most American UFOlogists. Unlike their desperate desire to unravel the medical secrets of devious, not to say even wicked, experimenters, Sprinkle claims that his evidence paints a much more positive light. That, in effect, his witnesses are not victims but the chosen few groomed as cosmic citizens. That is rather interesting, given what we have uncovered in this book.

Each year since 1980, at the University of Wyoming in Laramie, he brings them together for a 'Rocky Mountain convention'. The emotive power of so many potential star children in one place creates an exciting spiritual energy and probably contributes to his own theories about what is going on.

However, just as influential is likely to be the fact that, rather like me, Leo Sprinkle faced up to the challenge of odd memories within his own past. He explored from further via a fellow therapist and concluded that he too had been contacted. The doctor was a pawn in the grand chess game that UFO reality has become.

Leo Sprinkle has seen UFOs over Boulder, Colorado, the very town where the Condon team later pontificated.

These were in both 1949 and 1956. But when regressed to a child of about ten years old Sprinkle also found himself reliving a forgotten experience aboard a UFO with a tall Nordic entity standing next to him. The being explained how he must learn well at school because when the boy grew older his task was to help others come to terms with their purpose in life. From this Sprinkle graduated through university and post-grad work to become a counsellor with the life that he has today.

It scarcely matters whether this regression image was an allegorical dream or a real hidden memory of an actual spacenapping. What it undoubtedly became was a trigger that catapulted the psychologist into fulfilling a role – just as so many others who we would call star children have been propelled headlong, often unsuspecting, into their own unique destiny. The interlocking plan that seems to be behind these things is a marvel to behold.

Leo Sprinkle has a very definite view of what is going on, moulded by his own experience and his unique insight through so much contact with all these star children.

In 1990 he told the International Forum of New Science, held in Colorado, that there was a gradual escalation of acceptance of evidence. We could see that clearly through a history of the field.

Once lights in the sky were taboo, then they became accepted by the late 1940s. But sightings of alien craft were not credible, until by the mid-1950s these were acceptable too. More UFO types were replaced by the next step up the ladder – sightings of aliens, rejected until after the 1954 wave – and so on. This whole process has continued ever since, with alien contact experiencing baptisms aplenty before being replaced by yet another new trend.

I have been thinking about Sprinkle's perceptive comments and it makes sense of some niggling things that have bothered me about the subject for years. As each sub-phenomenon within the UFO field has reached a certain level of acceptance it has then just faded away and been taken over by a new, more extraordinary set of cases.

Why, for instance, do virtually all the credible, well-attested photographs of strange craft date back thirty or forty years? Camera ownership has tripled since 1955, quality of equipment and film stock has improved vastly. Yet I have seen the UFO photographic evidence that comes in day by day and cases like McMinnville, Oregon, (1950) and Trindade Island, Brazil (1957), have all but disappeared everywhere we look. Why?

If you think the answer is that these few good cases were fakes (although the evidence disputes it) and researchers now have better methods and would not be fooled so readily, that is not the point. For we are not even getting attempted hoaxes. Given the ease with which fakes could be engineered and the huge profile for UFOs these days we ought to be bombarded with pictures of strange craft – whether they are (and always were) real craft or trickery. The fact that they just don't turn up at all clearly argues for a fundamental change within the phenomenon itself.

The same is true of the stranger cases. They go through patterns – then, when that pattern is established, they vanish overnight. We do not see aliens landing and collecting rock samples like we used to do. We have almost no abductions without medical examinations these days. It is all just as if the evidence makes its point in some way then, once assured that this point has registered, plans the next move upward and starts a grand campaign to stuff this down humanity's throat – in the nicest possible way.

Of course, there could be psychological or sociological factors at work here – but this one step at a time manner of presenting the evidence to us is an undeniable force within the alien contact mystery which cries out for understanding. Yet it is all but being ignored by researchers.

If I understand Leo Sprinkle correctly, he sees this, rather as I do, as a kind of 'education programme'. After you pass through one grade it's time to graduate to the next school year. He says: 'I have considered the possibility that UFO activity is part of an educational program for "cosmic consciousness conditioning", and for assisting humankind to learn more about the merger of "science" and "spirituality".'

In other words, I think he means, and if he doesn't then

I certainly do, that a key point of what is going on is gradual persuasion and integration of the human mind into a much deeper and more spiritual form of awareness. Sprinkle seems to think this may be practised by the extraterrestrial originators of this entire contact programme.

Their plan is not to land on the White House lawn five minutes after crossing the galactic void, say 'Hello' and promptly get shot at by the US Air Force. It is instead a much more leisurely and (in their eyes) meaningful one of helping the human race to better itself. In effect it sets puzzles, throws down challenges, tests us with observation exercises which we must interact with and uses them to raise our own consciousness.

One thing that I learnt from teaching – the fundamental rule, in fact – is that if you have a bunch of kids and you want them to learn something that is above their heads and perhaps of minimal interest to them, then the last thing you do is sit them down and get them to learn this by rote or instruction. The end result of doing that would be that many will rebel and ignore the teaching and most of the rest will not comprehend a thing.

So what do you do? The best answer teaching has found is to lead them gradually through the stages that drew the great thinkers and pioneers towards this truth – one step at a time, taking their pace, not yours, and only moving onward when it is clear that they are ready as the previous step has been absorbed. Moreover, you teach abstract or uninteresting things by way of issues and illustrations that are relevant and which jump out and grab their attention. Everyone learns best when the lesson seems to be about a subject they enjoy – even when, beneath the surface, they may be unconsciously taking on board the real point of the exercise as well.

I actually used UFOs this way myself. If I wanted to teach some 12-year-olds about the weather, I got them talking about UFOs and thinking around how various phenomena might explain some of these. Because they loved UFO stories, they enjoyed all of this, hardly realizing that the topic of the day was meteorology rather than UFOlogy.

I suspect quite strongly that the entire mystery of alien contact is a giant school excursion for the human race. It teaches its lessons in pictorial form by posing fascinating teasers that pique our imagination. They keep us asking questions and force us to look beyond the little square box of solid reality that we have built around ourselves like a coffin.

It may well be that much of what we see – the minutiae of the experience – is of fairly minor consequence. What count are the changes that are gradually being instilled deep within ourselves. Dramatic adaptations of human consciousness are being engineered by the alien contact experience and we are not noticing all these lessons as we let ourselves be taken for a ride.

They do say that a spoonful of sugar helps the medicine go down and – just as Gary told Peter Warrington and I back in 1976 – this whole phenomenon may well be like that. It could be the lollipop that we suck on to take our minds off other things that may not taste quite as good but are of great importance nonetheless to our planetary future.

We use the word 'alien' regularly throughout this book, but also rather loosely. We are constrained to think of extraterrestrial Captain Kirks riding their version of the Starship Enterprise and coming to earth to 'explore strange new worlds and new civilizations and (forgive the split infinitive) boldly go where no alien has gone before'.

But that is a human concept. Aliens, if they exist, will be anything but human. Remember our problem with the dolphin interacting with human scientists. We don't have a clue how dolphins think, what dolphin society is like and yet we have shared this planet with them for millions of years. It is ludicrously presumptuous of us to assume that we could ever interpret the thoughts, actions and intentions of alien visitors who might therefore be behind the education programme or, indeed, the entire star child mystery.

Yet presume it we do, if only because we have this burning need to comprehend the incomprehensible.

Try remembering that the universe is, so far as we

know, infinite. It has no beginning and no end and simply is, was and forever will be. What is outside this vastness of space and time? Our mind strains under the attempts to define the impossible. We are just not equipped to handle such mega questions, yet we struggle to do it. So we come up with ideas about space curving back upon itself into a four-, five- or six-dimensional sphere. In truth it does little to dent our incredulity but it makes us feel better that we are at least making an effort. Mankind, in its arrogance, simply cannot bear to have things defeat its very ability to think about them.

This, I suspect, is why we impose human conditions on the UFO mystery. The Dan Dare names of the aliens, the human trappings of their UFOs, are probably all far more to do with our mind, its visual store of images and that desperation to pin the blame on something. They may have little connection with any true alien reality.

That, I fear, would be so alien we could not draw a ring around it – just as we cannot draw a lifelike picture of God, yet every society has always tried, e.g. with fluffy clouds and old men with white beards.

When ancient island civilizations – in the south Pacific, for instance – first encountered western technology they responded in exactly this way. They saw aircraft as 'big birds' – not just as a name applied to them – they literally *saw* them as big birds. Their minds had no image of air technology, so they could not perceive it. They only had familiarity as a culture with birds that lived within the sky, so the aircraft were reported with bird-like characteristics. This literally changed their appearance.

These people were not mistaken – as we might suggest they were. They were not blinkered and unable to see the truth. Their truth was as valid as ours. It was just different.

The way the human mind works is to take in concepts and clothe them in imagery which is plucked from the storehouse built of past experience. When something completely unexperienced in every conceivable way comes along then there is nothing the mind can do except picture it in familiar terms.

I believe that today we are the South Sea islanders. The alien contact experience is like those aeroplanes. We have absolutely no way to grasp the true content of this phenomenon because it is way beyond our comprehension and totally outside all our experience. So we see what exists in our minds.

In the past, we saw our UFOs as airships, which were at the forefront of technology in those days. Our modern UFOs are science-fiction spaceships and aliens simply because that reflects the cutting edge of today's society.

None of these things are what is *really* there. We waste almost all our time chasing phantoms and trying to figure out why alien examination tables are made of metal, entities' skins are coloured grey, or why their spaceships don't have lifts to move from floor to floor.

It is a bit like trying to understand the nature of fire by writing encyclopedias full of debate about the funny little shapes and pictures that our mind sees within the flickers of the flame. That may teach us something about ourselves, but it offers nothing really about the essence of fire itself. Yet fire is there and we respond to its side effects. We are just missing the significance in a fruitless search through irrelevancies.

I believe that we should react to our evidence rather like interpreters of dreams; seek the meaning behind the imagery. That is not to belittle this phenomenon, because I think that it is very important. Indeed, whether the contact comes from within ourselves, via some imaginal realm or is an alien force that we are not comprehending, there is a contact, and it is our responsibility to try to heed its message.

The night before I wrote this final chapter I had a vivid dream. It was just a dream, I am fairly sure of that, and it should be no great surprise that I had one like it after steeping myself in this subject for weeks on end whilst writing this book. But reporting the dream and seeking any message behind it is a worthwhile exercise, if only to demonstrate my point that we should focus less on perhaps illusory hard evidence and take better note of what we might call the soft side to the UFO mystery.

So, for what it is worth, here is what I dreamt one night in April 1994.

* * *

I was standing in open countryside looking up at a steely sky. As I stared, a round grey object popped into view out of nowhere. It was, of course, a classic UFO.

I felt a desperate longing to understand it – to go into it – to find out its purpose – even to be at home within it. Then, suddenly, I was. Some force had picked me up and transported me into this weird place.

Now I was inside a room. It was round and large but it was completely empty. There was no alien technology. No entities. Nothing. I felt really miserable that after all this effort, after snatching this great chance, I had arrived nowhere and with no sign of any answers.

Yet, at the same time, I was aware that there were aliens here. They were surrounding me and invisible, yet alongside me as well. I was trying to grasp the point of all this confusion. I can only describe it as if they were in the room but inside another dimension, so in my terms they were not in the room at all. Yet I could sense them, going about their business and ignoring me.

This was what hurt. I felt them say: 'What we are doing does not concern you. You would not understand it anyway.'

I must have looked a pathetic sight, miserable at being so close and yet so far from the truth. So they chose to humour me by asking me to look out of a window in the side of the craft. We were hovering low over some town and yet everybody was wandering about down below taking no notice of this huge thing above their rooftops. I could not understand and presumed they were simply not looking upwards. But then I understood. These people could not see us because we were in their frame of reality but they were not in ours. So far as they were concerned we did not exist.

Again the entities (whom I never actually saw) humoured me by briefly materializing into the reality of that town. I saw a man come out of a pub, look up at us with his face now aghast and then turn away. When he looked back we had evidently vanished again and he shook his head from side to side utterly confused. I knew that he was now in a hopeless mess and would remain so for the rest of his life. Nobody would believe the tale of a man coming out of a pub. He would probably grow not to believe it for himself. Yet for one brief moment he had been allowed to see a higher reality. He had just not been able to understand what had happened to him.

Then I saw that my position was exactly the same. Who could I tell about what I was experiencing now? It was like trying to make somebody experience your dream. They could not do it, because that dream was for you.

I looked back and the aliens had already returned to their netherworld doing whatever it was that they were doing. I had been a fleeting distraction – not the main point of what they were up to. What I had seen happen was just a side effect of true reality, which continued unabated all around me and remained far beyond my ability to see it.

Then I knew that I had to go and, in an instant, I was back on the street and the UFO had vanished. I felt a strange cocktail of emotions – like nostalgia. There was sadness, disappointment, excitement and challenge. For I knew that I had to somehow convey the magic of the impossible to others.

Like my dream, I think the alien contact mystery is a mandala – an image upon which we meditate to alter and raise our state of consciousness.

I do not mean that mystically, or, then again, perhaps I do. What I am striving to say is that the mystery exists *because* it is a mystery. It conveys something deep inside like an intravenous injection straight into the soul. It teases and tantalizes our limited consciousness, forcing us to look upwards and outwards for greater perception.

We are being gradually turned into star children – or, as Sprinkle calls them, cosmic citizens, or, indeed, as Ring would have it, Omega people. Names do not matter. Understanding is what counts.

This experience exists despite us and because of us. It surrounds us and immerses us, bathing every thinking person in the heady scent of true reality. For the world is a stranger place than most of us can possibly imagine and the universe is infinitely stranger still.

That is what we are being taught by all of this. We are climbing a stairway to the stars with a dazzling light far ahead of us at the top. We do not know where we are going, or why we have to go there, but we know that it is a journey as inevitable as life itself.

Some of us will inch our way little by little. Others will sit back and ride upon the treadle as it climbs ever upward to reach its goal. A few may take the stairs in leaps and bounds, several at a time, unprepared to wait for the mechanism to get them there at its own speed. They may even slip and fall back down again, accepting that as the price to pay for over-enthusiasm. One or two may need a helping hand to get anywhere at all, or like dogs on an escalator, will need to be picked up and carried because they are frozen by panic into statuesque immobility.

None of this matters. Each to their own special way. We will all get there in the end. And when we do arrive, I suspect we might well find that our joy is short-lived. For we are only on the first floor of a very tall building.

Appendix

Are You a Star Child?

Star children could be all around us. You may be one yourself. Your husband or wife might be, or one of your children. How can we tell?

There is no foolproof way, but here are some clues to look out for that might help you to decide. Which of these seem to apply?

Treat these questions seriously. Do not respond in a flippant manner and do not answer yes if you do not really mean it or just because you want to be a star child. Be warned – safeguards have been designed against precisely that possibility!

I would suggest that you do not answer these questions about yourself. By all means ask them of your spouse or child, but avoid using this as a self-questionnaire wherever that is possible.

If you are brave enough, you could ask someone close to you to fill in the answers about you, or you could get a trusted friend to ask them of you.

Good luck!

1   Do you have any unusual phobias; such as fears of certain colours or a reaction to a particular word?

2   When out driving or walking is there an area that you will make a long detour to avoid, even if you are not conscious of why you are doing so?

3   Have you seen what you are pretty certain was a UFO on more than one occasion – if so, how often?

4   Have you had a number of vivid dreams about aliens and UFOs?

5   Do you dream normally in colour and recall at least two or three dreams every night? Have you had flying, floating or lucid dreams?

6   When you read the words Sobec-alp do they create any unusual feelings? What kind of feelings?

7   Did you develop a sudden intense interest in the following: space, ecology, antiquity, psychic phenomena, the sea, mysticism or fountains?

8   At what age did you have the earliest vivid memory that you can check for accuracy with other family members?

9   As a child did you ever experience, or talk to your family about, strange figures or odd light effects appearing in your bedroom?

10   Between the ages of three and ten did you ever believe that your wardrobe could move or even talk to you?

11   Do you have an interest in, or enjoy attempting, poetry, creative writing, chess, logic puzzles or art?

12   Have you ever had periods in your life when more than half an hour of time – or some awareness of space and distance – has disappeared and you cannot remember how or why?

Please feel free to submit your answers. You can do so anonymously if you wish and elaborate as much as you want upon any point. But please give your age, sex and whether the questions were self-answered or not.

Also, please feel free to contact me to describe your own UFO or alien experiences (ask for confidentiality if you prefer). If you would like to be put in touch with a trusted researcher so as to pursue your story further, then just ask.

Jenny Randles, c/o 37 Heathbank Road, Stockport, Cheshire, England SK3 OUP.

References

The MIT proceedings are, as of mid-1994, still not available, although long promised. One of the specialist booksellers listed at the end of these references will tell you if this important document is now on sale.

My own books referred to in the text are as follows:

UFOs: A British Viewpoint (with Peter Warrington), Robert Hale, 1979
The Pennine UFO Mystery, Grafton, 1983
UFO Reality, Robert Hale, 1983
Science and the UFOs (with Peter Warrington), Blackwell, 1986
Sixth Sense, Robert Hale, 1987
Abduction, Robert Hale, 1988
Mind Monsters, Aquarian, 1990
Crop Circles: A Mystery Solved (with Paul Fuller), Robert Hale, 1993
Aliens: The Real Story, Robert Hale, 1994

Other texts of relevance:

Flying Saucers: A Modern Myth, Jung, Dr Carl, Routledge, 1959
Scientific Study of UFOs, Condon, Dr E. (ed), Bantam, 1969
Life After Life, Moody, Dr Ray, Bantam, 1975
The Andreasson Affair, Fowler, Ray, Prentice-Hall, 1979
UFOs: The Image Hypothesis, Basterfield, Keith, Reed, 1980
The Interrupted Journey, Fuller, John, Souvenir, 1980

Andreasson Affair: Phase Two, Fowler, Ray, Prentice-Hall, 1982

Terror That Comes by Night, Hufford, David, Univ. of Penn., 1982

Missing Time, Hopkins, Budd, Merak, 1982

Aliens Among Us, Montgomery, Ruth, Ballantine, 1985

Communion, Strieber, Whitley, Century, 1987

Intruders, Hopkins, Budd, Random House, 1987

Perspectives, Spencer, John, McDonald, 1989

The Watchers, Fowler, Ray, Bantam, 1990

The Omega Project, Ring, Dr Kenneth, Morrow, 1992

Secret Life, Jacobs, Dr David, Fourth Estate, 1993

Publications

The Dr J. Allen Hynek Center for UFO studies publish the *International UFO Reporter* and the *Journal of UFO Studies*: 2457 West Peterson Ave, Chicago, Illinois, IL 60659, USA

The Mutual UFO Network, of which HUFON is an affiliate, publish *MUFON Journal*: 103 Oldtowne Road, Seguin, Texas, TX 78155-4099, USA

UFO Research Australia coordinate most serious research work in that country: PO Box 229, Prospect, South Australia 5082

The *Bulletin of Anomalous Experience* is the best source of up-to-date commentary and discussion on spacenapping phenomena: Dr David Gotlib, 2 St Clair Ave West, Suite 607, Toronto, M4V 1LF, Canada

Cynthia Hind collates information from the African continent and publishes UFO Afrinews semi-regularly: Gemini, PO Box MP49, Mount Pleasant, Harare, Zimbabwe

In Britain, many groups in the North, Midlands and Scotland work via an alliance called NUFON (Northern UFO Network) and publish *Northern UFO News*. Details via NARO (Northern Anomalies Research Organisation): 37 Heathbank Rd, Stockport, Cheshire, SK3 OUP

Mail order catalogues of all the latest titles and availability of books and magazines is offered c/o Spacelink Books, 115 Hollybush Lane, Hampton, Middlesex, TW12 2QY; Arcturus Books, 1443 SE Port St Lucie Boulvd, Port St Lucie, FL 34952, USA; Sydney Esoteric, 475-9 Elizabeth St, Surry Hills, NSW 2010, Australia

Second-hand books – often the only way to get titles more than two or three years old – can be purchased – again by mail order – via Midnight Books, The Mount, Ascerton Rd, Sidmouth, Devon, EX10 9BT

Readers in Britain (only) can get the latest information about UFOs and alien contacts, updated each weekend, on UFO Call – a news service operated via British Telecom by BUFORA (British UFO Research Association). Jenny Randles has written and presented this service since 1989. It is offered at the normal premium charges for information lines: UFO Call 0891 12 18 86

A new venture was launched by a group of British UFOlogists in June 1994. The *New UFOlogist* is unique: a non-profit magazine tied to no organisation, but offering high-quality research. All money raised will form a central fund to which anyone can submit a request for grant aid to develop either a detailed case study or research proposal. The administration of the fund will be in the hands of open meetings to which all interested participants will be invited. The *New UFOlogist* is available from: 71 Knight Avenue, Canterbury, Kent, CT2 8PY.

Index